ULTIMATE TRIVIA

1400+ MIND-BLOWING FACTS FOR CURIOUS PEOPLE

BEN DOUGLAS

ANCIENT & HISTORICAL EVENTS

UNSOLVED & MYSTERIOUS EVENTS

LANGUAGE & COMMUNICATION

CRIME & JUSTICE

SPORTS

RECORD-BREAKING ACHIEVEMENTS

ANIMALS & PETS

FOOD & DAILY LIFE

THE UNITED STATES

DOOMSDAY & SURVIVAL

ART & CREATIVITY

INTRODUCTION

Did you know the CIA once tried to turn ordinary house cats into spies? Or that behind Mount Rushmore, hidden inside Abraham Lincoln's stone head, there's a secret room where historical documents rest in a titanium vault? Here's another surprise—one of the wealthiest men in the world still lives in the same modest house he bought in 1958, and eats the same $3.17 McDonald's breakfast every single morning.

Welcome to a remarkable journey through history's most fascinating secrets, where each story challenges what we think we know about the world. This isn't just another collection of facts—it's a treasury of tales that will change how you see things forever.

From the glamorous world of Old Hollywood to the marvels of modern engineering, from Wild West adventures to behind-the-scenes presidential secrets, these pages hold stories that will make you pause and say, **"Wait... really?"** These are the kinds of discoveries you'll want to share with friends and family, the conversations that begin with **"You won't believe what I just learned..."**

Each chapter reveals a new world of wonders. You'll meet the U.S. President who held important meetings while sitting on the toilet—door wide open—because he refused to waste a single minute of his day. You'll discover how lucky accidents changed the world, how small choices shaped major historical events, and how the words we use every day tell surprising stories about human creativity and occasional silliness.

What makes these stories truly special isn't just their power to surprise—it's how they show us the amazing variety of human experience. Behind every unusual fact lies a deeper story: about people solving problems in creative ways, about luck meeting preparation, about human nature in all its wonderful strangeness.

Get ready to be amazed and delighted. Whether you love learning new things, enjoy telling stories, or simply like being surprised, you'll find yourself coming back to these pages again and again.

After all, we live in a world where sunflowers are actually thousands of tiny flowers pretending to be one big flower, where America's shortest president weighed just 100 pounds, and where a loyal dog earned its own star on the Hollywood Walk of Fame. Sometimes real life is more incredible than anything we could imagine.

Turn the page, and let's discover these wonderful stories together.

Ben Douglas

POPULAR TELEVISION SHOWS

⊚ *I Love Lucy* (1951–1957) was the first television show to be filmed in front of a live studio audience. Desi Arnaz pioneered the use of multiple cameras, a technique that became the industry standard for sitcoms.

⊚ *I Dream of Jeannie* had to carefully film Barbara Eden's belly button out of sight. NBC censors considered showing a navel too risqué for 1960s television.

⊚ *The Twilight Zone* (1959–1964) was one of the first TV shows to feature African American actors in non-stereotypical roles. Rod Serling, the show's creator, insisted on tackling social issues despite pushback from network executives.

⊚ *Star Trek* (1966–1969) was one of the first American shows to depict an interracial kiss. The historic scene between Captain Kirk and Lieutenant Uhura nearly didn't happen due to network concerns but was ultimately aired.

⊚ *Twin Peaks* was such a massive pop culture hit in its first season that the question "Who killed Laura Palmer?" became a national obsession. However, when the mystery was solved early in Season 2, ratings plummeted, leading to the show's early cancellation.

◎ *The Simpsons* (1989–present) is the longest-running primetime scripted series in U.S. history. The show predicted multiple real-world events, including Donald Trump's presidency and Disney's purchase of Fox.

◎ *Friends* (1994–2004) wasn't always supposed to be called *Friends*—early titles included *Insomnia Café* and *Six of One*. The cast members negotiated their contracts together, ensuring equal pay for all six stars.

◎ Before becoming an international superstar, Clint Eastwood played Rowdy Yates on *Rawhide*. His low-budget cowboy hat was so cheap that it would droop in the rain, forcing frequent replacements.

◎ *Breaking Bad* (2008–2013) was originally planned as a single-season show. AMC extended it after realizing Bryan Cranston's performance was too good to end so soon.

◎ *Game of Thrones* (2011–2019) once filmed ten hours of extras walking in circles to create the massive battle sequence in "Battle of the Bastards." The grueling shoot resulted in one of the most realistic medieval combat scenes ever put on screen.

◎ *The Office* (U.S., 2005–2013) was nearly canceled after its first season due to poor ratings. However, after Netflix picked it up for streaming, it became one of the most-watched shows of the 2010s.

◎ *M*A*S*H* (1972–1983) had a series finale that was watched by over 105 million people, making it the most-watched scripted television episode in U.S. history. The show lasted nearly four times longer than the Korean War it depicted.

◎ *Seinfeld* (1989–1998) was originally described as a "show about nothing." In reality, many of its bizarre plotlines were based on true stories from the lives of the show's writers.

◎ *Stranger Things* (2016–present) was inspired by 1980s pop culture, particularly *E.T.*, *The Goonies*, and *Stephen King* novels. Eleven's character was loosely based on a real-life government experiment known as MKUltra.

◎ *Columbo* was one of the first shows to reveal the murderer at the beginning of each episode. Instead of a "whodunit," the show focused on *how* the detective would catch the killer, making it a unique take on the crime genre.

◎ *Cheers* (1982–1993) had such low ratings in its first season that NBC nearly canceled it. By its final season, it was one of the highest-rated shows on television.

◎ *The Fresh Prince of Bel-Air* (1990–1996) was loosely based on the life of Benny Medina, a music executive. Will Smith had never acted before the show and memorized the entire script, often mouthing other actors' lines.

◎ *The Mary Tyler Moore Show* was groundbreaking for depicting a single, independent woman with a career. CBS executives worried viewers would assume Mary Richards was divorced, so they made her a "career woman" instead of a divorcée.

◎ *Doctor Who* (1963–present) holds the Guinness World Record for the longest-running sci-fi television series. The Doctor's ability to regenerate was introduced to keep the show going after the first actor, William Hartnell, became too ill to continue.

◎ *The Walking Dead* (2010–2022) originally planned to kill off Rick Grimes much earlier, but Andrew Lincoln's performance changed the writers' minds. The show also used real animal intestines for some zombie scenes.

◎ *Star Trek: The Next Generation* almost had completely different uniforms. The original concept featured tunic-style outfits with no pants, but the cast hated them, leading to the now-iconic fitted Starfleet uniforms.

◎ *Lost* (2004–2010) was inspired by *Survivor* and *Cast Away*. The writers originally planned to kill off Jack Shephard in the first episode, but test audiences hated the idea.

⊚ *The Sopranos* (1999–2007) was the first cable TV series to win an Emmy for Outstanding Drama Series. The show's controversial final scene, cutting to black mid-action, still sparks debates today.

⊚ *Fantasy Island* and *The Love Boat* had a surprising connection—both shows featured a rotating cast of celebrity guest stars. ABC intentionally scheduled them back-to-back to create a "guest star showcase" on Saturday nights.

⊚ *Buffy the Vampire Slayer* (1997–2003) was one of the first TV shows to feature a season-long story arc. It also broke ground with its LGBTQ+ representation, with Willow and Tara's relationship being one of TV's first same-sex romances.

⊚ *South Park* (1997–present) was created using construction paper cutouts before switching to digital animation. The show is produced in just six days per episode, allowing for rapid responses to current events.

⊚ *Dexter* (2006–2013, 2021) was partially inspired by real-life serial killer Pedro Rodrigues Filho. The show's dark yet humorous tone helped redefine the antihero in television.

⊚ *The X-Files* (1993–2018) popularized the phrase "The Truth Is Out There." The show's eerie theme music was created by accident when the composer accidentally left his hand on an echo effect.

⊚ The iconic opening of *Get Smart*, where Maxwell Smart walks through a series of automated doors, was filmed at an actual aircraft hangar. The doors were real, not just a set piece.

⊚ *How I Met Your Mother* (2005–2014) filmed its final scene with Ted's kids in advance to prevent the actors from aging. The show's ending was planned from the beginning, but it still divided fans.

⊚ *The Golden Girls* (1985–1992) featured Betty White, who was originally cast as Blanche before swapping roles with Rue McClanahan. The show's kitchen set was later reused in *Gilmore Girls*.

⊚ *Supernatural* (2005–2020) holds the record as the longest-running American sci-fi/fantasy series. The show was originally planned to last only five seasons but ran for 15 due to its devoted fanbase.

⊚ The producers of *The Andy Griffith Show* deliberately never mentioned what state Mayberry was in. Fans have long speculated it was North Carolina, based on Griffith's real-life hometown of Mount Airy.

⊚ *House* (2004–2012) was inspired by Sherlock Holmes, with Dr. House's name being a reference to Holmes (House = Home = Holmes). His street address in the show was also 221B, just like the famous detective's.

⊚ *Parks and Recreation* (2009–2015) was initially meant to be a *The Office* spin-off. Leslie Knope was originally written as a clueless character, but Amy Poehler's charisma led the writers to make her more competent.

⊚ *CSI: Crime Scene Investigation* (2000–2015) led to a phenomenon called "The CSI Effect," where real-life jurors expected forensic evidence in every case, leading to difficulties in actual trials.

⊚ *Glee* (2009–2015) broke a record for most songs charting on the Billboard Hot 100, surpassing Elvis Presley and The Beatles. The show's musical numbers often outsold actual pop stars' singles.

⊚ *The Big Bang Theory* (2007–2019) paid a real physicist, David Saltzberg, to ensure all scientific references were accurate. The show's theme song was written by Barenaked Ladies specifically for the series.

⊚ *Brooklyn Nine-Nine* (2013–2021) was saved by NBC after Fox canceled it due to fan outcry. The show is one of the few police comedies to tackle real-world issues like racial profiling.

⊚ *Frasier* (1993–2004) holds the record for the most Emmy wins for a sitcom. Kelsey Grammer played Frasier Crane for 20 years across two series, making it one of TV's longest-running characters.

⊚ *Sherlock* (2010–2017) was written to modernize Arthur Conan Doyle's stories, with Benedict Cumberbatch's fast-talking deduction scenes becoming iconic. The show's writers are the same duo behind *Doctor Who*.

◎ *E.R.* (1994–2009) launched George Clooney's career. The show was originally a movie script written by Michael Crichton, the author of *Jurassic Park*.

◎ *The Mandalorian* (2019–present) revolutionized TV production with its use of "The Volume," a massive LED screen that creates realistic backgrounds in real-time, reducing the need for location shoots.

TELEVISION HISTORY

◎ Television signals travel at the speed of light, meaning broadcasts from Earth are still moving through space. If aliens had televisions, they could be watching *I Love Lucy* right now—assuming they're about 70 light-years away.

◎ The first-ever television broadcast took place in 1928 when W3XK, an experimental station in Washington, D.C., aired a test pattern. The image was a simple spinning silhouette of a puppet named Felix the Cat.

◎ The world's first electronic television was invented by Philo Farnsworth in 1927 when he successfully transmitted a simple straight line. Farnsworth was just 21 years old at the time and had been developing the idea since he was a teenager.

◎ The first remote control for a television, called the "Lazy Bones," was introduced by Zenith in 1950. It was connected to the TV by a long wire, which people frequently tripped over.

◎ The first wireless remote control, the "Flash-Matic," used a beam of light to change channels. However, sunlight often interfered with it, accidentally flipping channels or turning the TV on and off.

◎ In 1936, the BBC became the first network to broadcast a regularly scheduled television service. However, programming was so limited that the network would sometimes just show a clock ticking.

◎ The first television commercial aired in 1941 for Bulova watches. It cost only $9 to air and lasted just 10 seconds, displaying the slogan, "America runs on Bulova time."

◎ The first color television broadcast in the U.S. occurred in 1951, featuring a variety show called *Premiere*. However, most people still owned black-and-white sets, so they watched in grayscale.

◎ The first home televisions were so small that people often used magnifying glasses to enlarge the image. Some early sets had screens only five inches wide, smaller than many modern smartphones.

◎ The 1969 moon landing was the most-watched television broadcast of its time, with over 600 million people tuning in. Neil Armstrong's first steps were captured using a camera specifically designed to survive extreme temperatures on the lunar surface.

◎ Television was originally thought to be a passing fad, much like radio dramas. In 1939, a New York Times article even dismissed TV as an impractical technology that would never catch on.

◎ The TV dinner was invented in 1953 when Swanson overestimated how much turkey Americans would eat for Thanksgiving. They repackaged the leftovers in aluminum trays and marketed them as meals people could eat while watching television.

◎ The first televised presidential debate in 1960 between John F. Kennedy and Richard Nixon changed the course of politics. Radio listeners thought Nixon won, but TV viewers favored Kennedy, who appeared more confident and composed under the lights.

◎ Before digital screens, televisions used cathode-ray tubes (CRTs), which fired electrons at a phosphorescent screen to create images. This is why older TVs had a curved shape and weighed as much as a small car.

⊚ The first live TV broadcast of an atomic bomb test occurred in 1952. The explosion, known as *Operation Ivy Mike*, was so powerful that it vaporized an entire island in the Pacific.

⊚ The term "soap opera" comes from the fact that early daytime dramas were sponsored by soap companies. Shows like *Guiding Light* were originally created as a way to sell more detergent to housewives.

⊚ In 1971, cigarette ads were banned from American television. The final cigarette commercial aired during *The Tonight Show Starring Johnny Carson* just before the ban took effect at midnight.

⊚ The world's first high-definition TV broadcast happened in Japan in 1989. However, early HD televisions were so expensive that only a handful of people could afford them.

⊚ Before digital TV, if you turned on a channel with no signal, the static you saw—often called "snow"—was partially caused by cosmic radiation left over from the Big Bang. In a way, watching static meant seeing the remnants of the universe's birth.

⊚ The invention of the VCR in the 1970s terrified television networks, which feared people would record shows and skip commercials. The Supreme Court ruled in 1984 that home recording was legal, paving the way for modern streaming.

⊚ The phrase "binge-watching" was first used in the early 2000s but exploded in popularity with the rise of Netflix. Before streaming, people would "binge-watch" by buying DVD box sets of their favorite shows.

⊚ John Ritter's physical comedy in *Three's Company* was so extreme that he once suffered a groin injury from one of his famous pratfalls. Despite the pain, he continued filming with barely a break.

⊚ The first reality TV show aired in 1973—*An American Family* on PBS. The documentary-style show followed the lives of the Loud family and shocked viewers when the parents' divorce played out on screen.

◎ The average American household had only one TV in the 1950s. By the 1990s, most homes had at least three televisions, making the TV more common than an indoor bathroom in some places.

◎ Closed captions were first introduced in 1972 to make television accessible to the hearing impaired. The technology paved the way for subtitles in multiple languages, changing the way people watch TV worldwide.

◎ Television signals once traveled through the airwaves using antennas, but by 2009, the U.S. completely transitioned to digital broadcasting. This meant that old "rabbit ears" antennas stopped working unless connected to a converter box.

◎ The longest-running TV news program, *Meet the Press*, has been on air since 1947. Originally, it was just a radio show, but it transitioned to television and has remained a Sunday morning staple ever since.

◎ The first television satellites were launched in the 1960s, allowing for live international broadcasts. The famous *Our World* program in 1967 linked 14 countries together, with The Beatles performing *All You Need Is Love* live for the world.

◎ The first time people could pause live TV was in 1999 when TiVo introduced the digital video recorder (DVR). The ability to skip commercials forever changed how advertisers approached television.

◎ In the 1980s, Japan experimented with "smell-o-vision," attempting to broadcast scents alongside television programs. The idea never caught on, but it remains one of the strangest TV-related experiments in history.

HISTORY OF TOYS

◎ The oldest known toy is a 4,000-year-old rattle found in Turkey. Made of baked clay with tiny stones inside, it shows that even ancient babies needed entertainment.

◎ The first dolls date back to at least 2000 BCE. Archaeologists have found wooden, ivory, and even wax dolls in ancient Egyptian tombs, some with moveable limbs and wigs made of real hair.

◎ The yo-yo is one of the oldest toys still played with today. It originated in ancient Greece around 500 BCE and was even used in some cultures as a hunting weapon before becoming a child's pastime.

◎ The first jigsaw puzzle was invented in the 1760s by British cartographer John Spilsbury. He glued a map onto wood, cut it into pieces, and used it as a teaching tool for geography students.

◎ The modern teddy bear was inspired by a real event involving President Theodore Roosevelt. After he refused to shoot a tied-up bear on a hunting trip, a toy shop owner created a stuffed bear in his honor— and "Teddy's bear" became an instant hit.

◎ Play-Doh was originally invented as a wallpaper cleaner. In the 1950s, when demand for the cleaner dropped, it was repurposed as a children's toy, launching one of the most iconic modeling compounds in history.

◎ The first building blocks for children were created in the 17th century by educator John Locke, who believed play could be educational. Over time, they evolved into modern wooden blocks and eventually LEGO bricks.

◎ The first mass-produced board game in the United States was *The Checkered Game of Life*, created by Milton Bradley in 1860. It was a morality-based game that rewarded players for virtues like honesty and hard work.

◎ Slinky was invented by accident in 1943 when an engineer named Richard James was working on tension springs for naval equipment. When one of the springs "walked" down a shelf, he realized it would make a fun toy.

◎ Mr. Potato Head was the first toy ever advertised on television in 1952. Originally, it was just a set of plastic facial features meant to be stuck into real potatoes—until parents complained about the rotting vegetables.

◎ The Rubik's Cube was invented in 1974 by Hungarian architect Ernö Rubik, but it was originally called the "Magic Cube." It took Rubik a month to solve his own puzzle after he scrambled it for the first time.

◎ The Etch A Sketch was originally called the "Télécran" and was developed in France in 1959. The Ohio Art Company bought the rights, renamed it, and launched it in the U.S.—where it became a holiday sensation almost overnight.

◎ Barbie made her debut in 1959, inspired by a German doll called *Bild Lilli* that was originally sold as an adult novelty item. Mattel redesigned her for children, and she became one of the best-selling toys of all time.

◎ The Easy-Bake Oven was introduced in 1963 and originally used a regular light bulb as its heating element. Despite its simple design, it was powerful enough to bake tiny cakes and cookies.

⊚ The first action figure was G.I. Joe, released in 1964. It was deliberately called an "action figure" instead of a doll to appeal to boys, creating a whole new toy category.

⊚ Hot Wheels debuted in 1968, designed by a General Motors car designer to roll faster and smoother than standard toy cars. Their revolutionary low-friction axles set them apart from Matchbox, their biggest competitor.

⊚ The Frisbee was originally a pie tin from the Frisbie Baking Company in Connecticut. College students discovered that the empty tins could be tossed through the air, and a toy company later transformed them into the plastic disc we know today.

⊚ The Super Soaker was created in 1989 by a NASA engineer named Lonnie Johnson. He originally designed it as a heat pump but realized it had potential as the most powerful water gun ever made.

⊚ The first Nerf ball was introduced in 1969 with the slogan "You can't damage lamps or break windows!" It was so popular that the brand expanded into foam darts, blasters, and a whole arsenal of soft projectiles.

⊚ The game *Twister* was nearly rejected by retailers because it required players to get too physically close. It only became a hit after Johnny Carson played it on *The Tonight Show* in 1966.

⊚ The first LEGO bricks were designed in 1949, but they weren't the interlocking kind we know today. The modern "stud-and-tube" system was patented in 1958, making the bricks lock together securely.

⊚ The Slip 'N Slide was invented in 1961 by a father who saw his son sliding across a wet concrete driveway. He sewed vinyl sheets together, attached a hose, and created one of the most famous summer toys of all time.

⊚ The first video game console, the Magnavox Odyssey, was released in 1972. It came with translucent screen overlays because it couldn't generate color graphics on its own.

◎ The Tamagotchi craze of the 90s almost didn't happen. Bandai executives were unsure if people would want a digital pet, but after a test launch in Japan, they became a global sensation.

◎ The yo-yo had a major revival in the 1920s thanks to a Filipino immigrant named Pedro Flores. He mass-produced the toy in the U.S., popularizing the modern yo-yo as a skill-based toy.

◎ The original Monopoly game was based on an earlier game called *The Landlord's Game*, created in 1904 to teach the dangers of wealth inequality. Ironically, Monopoly became one of the best-selling games of all time.

◎ Stretch Armstrong, the super-stretchy action figure, was filled with corn syrup to make him flexible. If punctured, the sticky liquid inside would ooze out, ruining the toy.

◎ The View-Master, introduced in 1939, was initially designed as a way to view scenic photographs in 3D. It later became a beloved children's toy with reels featuring cartoons, movies, and TV shows.

◎ The original Lite-Brite set came with small, sharp pegs that kids could easily lose—or step on. It was one of the first toys to combine creativity with illumination, inspiring later toys like the Gloworm and fiber optic lamps.

HUMAN EVOLUTION

◎ Your pinky toe is disappearing. As humans evolved to rely less on gripping with their feet, the little toe became smaller and weaker. Some scientists believe it may shrink further or even disappear in the distant future.

◎ Early humans almost went extinct. Around 70,000 years ago, a catastrophic volcanic eruption (Toba supereruption) may have reduced the human population to as few as 1,000 individuals, nearly wiping us out. Genetic evidence suggests we all descend from this small, lucky group of survivors.

◎ We still carry DNA from other human species. Modern humans inherited genes from Neanderthals and Denisovans through ancient interbreeding. If you have European or Asian ancestry, up to 2% of your DNA may be Neanderthal, while some Southeast Asians carry Denisovan genes that help with high-altitude survival.

◎ Your wisdom teeth are an evolutionary leftover. Early humans had larger jaws to handle a tough diet of raw plants and meat, but as cooking and food preparation evolved, our jaws shrank—yet our third molars stuck around, often causing painful problems.

⊚ Human babies are born "early" compared to other primates. Our large brains mean we need a longer development period, but if we stayed in the womb as long as other mammals do proportionally, human pregnancies would last about 21 months! Instead, babies finish much of their brain development outside the womb.

⊚ Neanderthals had bigger brains than us. Despite their reputation as primitive, Neanderthals actually had slightly larger brains than modern humans. However, their brain structure may have focused more on vision and body control rather than social complexity.

⊚ Some people have extra muscles that ancient humans needed. A small percentage of people still have the palmaris longus, a muscle in the forearm that helped early humans climb trees. You can check by touching your thumb to your pinky and flexing your wrist—if a tendon pops up, you have one!

⊚ Goosebumps are a useless survival tool—now. Our ancestors used them to puff up their body hair when cold or frightened, making them appear larger to predators. Since we lost most of our body hair, goosebumps are now just a quirky vestige of the past.

⊚ Humans almost evolved with venom. Some scientists believe an ancient ancestor of primates had venomous saliva, like modern slow lorises. Traces of venom-related genes still exist in our DNA, but they became inactive over millions of years.

⊚ Your brain is actually shrinking. Over the last 30,000 years, the average human brain has shrunk by about 10%. Some theories suggest it's because we rely more on social cooperation and technology rather than brute intelligence for survival.

⊚ Early humans walked further in a year than most of us do in a lifetime. Hunter-gatherers often traveled 9-15 miles per day, covering thousands of miles annually. Today, the average person walks less than 2 miles a day.

⊚ Your body remembers being a fish. The human embryo briefly develops gill-like structures, a tail, and a yolk sac during early development—remnants of our deep evolutionary past. These features disappear before birth, but they reveal our origins.

◎ Neanderthals could talk—but their voices were different. Evidence suggests Neanderthals had a vocal range similar to ours but may have spoken with a higher-pitched, nasal voice due to their anatomy. Their language skills were likely complex, though we'll never know exactly how they sounded.

◎ Some people have a hole near their ear—a leftover from fish ancestors. About 1% of people are born with a tiny hole near their ear, known as a preauricular sinus. It's thought to be an evolutionary remnant of gill-like structures in early vertebrates.

◎ Humans are the only primates without a bone in their penis. Most mammals, including our closest relatives like chimpanzees, have a baculum (penis bone). It's unclear why we lost ours, but one theory suggests it evolved due to monogamous mating habits.

◎ Your jaw size is shrinking, but your teeth aren't. Over time, human jaws have become smaller due to changes in diet, but our teeth haven't kept up with the evolution—leading to overcrowding, crooked teeth, and the need for braces.

◎ Ancient humans domesticated themselves. Unlike other animals we domesticated, humans evolved to be less aggressive, more cooperative, and have smaller faces over time. This process, known as "self-domestication," is linked to our ability to form complex societies.

◎ You still carry genes for a tail. Human embryos briefly grow a tail in the womb, but the genes for a full tail are still present in our DNA. Occasionally, babies are born with small tail-like appendages, a rare throwback to our evolutionary history.

◎ Blue eyes didn't exist 10,000 years ago. All humans originally had brown eyes until a single genetic mutation in Europe led to the first blue-eyed person. Every blue-eyed person today can trace their ancestry back to that individual.

◎ Your hands are built like a chimp's—but stronger. While our closest primate relatives have longer fingers for climbing, human hands evolved to grip tools and weapons with a stronger precision grip. This ability helped drive technological advancement.

◎ Hair color evolved for survival. Blond hair evolved in northern climates to help people absorb more sunlight, while darker hair protected against UV damage near the equator. Red hair, the rarest, is linked to adaptations for cold, cloudy environments.

◎ You still have caveman instincts. Despite modern life, your brain is wired for survival, making you crave high-calorie foods, fear the dark, and react to sudden movement—remnants of a past where these instincts kept us alive.

◎ The first "modern" humans were African travelers. Every person outside Africa today descends from a small group of humans who left the continent around 60,000 years ago. Their journey led to the spread of human civilization across the world.

◎ Neanderthals made jewelry. Far from being brutish cave-dwellers, Neanderthals created necklaces and decorated themselves with shells, bones, and pigments. Some pieces of jewelry found in caves predate the earliest Homo sapiens art.

◎ Humans are the only primates with a chin. No other animal has a true chin, and scientists still debate why we evolved one. Some think it helps with speech, while others believe it reinforces the jaw against the stress of chewing.

◎ Ancient humans wrestled saber-toothed cats. Fossil evidence suggests early humans fought off massive Ice Age predators, sometimes scavenging their kills. Some even used their bones and teeth for tools and ornaments.

◎ Your sweat smells different from a chimp's. Humans evolved more sweat glands than most primates, making us the best long-distance runners in the animal kingdom. The downside? Our sweat produces more bacteria, creating body odor.

◎ Ancient humans hibernated like bears. Some fossilized skeletons show signs of seasonal bone growth disruptions, suggesting early humans in cold regions may have entered a hibernation-like state to survive harsh winters.

◎ We are still evolving. Traits like lactose tolerance, disease resistance, and even shrinking brains show that human evolution is ongoing. The future human may look different from us—just as we look different from our ancestors 100,000 years ago.

MIND & BODY

◎ The human brain generates enough electrical energy to power a small light bulb. Even when you're asleep, your brain remains highly active, processing information and solidifying memories.

◎ Your body replaces its entire skeleton about every 10 years. Bone cells are constantly breaking down and rebuilding, ensuring your skeleton stays strong and adaptable.

◎ The average person blinks about 15-20 times per minute, adding up to roughly 14,000 blinks per day. Blinking not only keeps your eyes lubricated but also gives your brain micro-breaks to process information.

◎ Your heart beats about 100,000 times per day, pumping roughly 2,000 gallons of blood through your body. Over a lifetime, that's enough to fill more than three Olympic-sized swimming pools.

◎ The gut and brain are so closely connected that the digestive system is often called the "second brain." Your gut contains about 500 million neurons, which communicate with your brain via the vagus nerve, influencing emotions, stress levels, and even decision-making.

◎ A single human hair can support up to 100 grams of weight—roughly the weight of two Hershey's chocolate bars. In theory, if all the hairs on your head were strong enough and distributed evenly, they could support the weight of an adult.

◎ Laughter triggers the release of endorphins, reducing stress and increasing pain tolerance. Some studies suggest that 15 minutes of laughter can burn up to 40 calories—though it's not quite enough to skip the gym.

◎ Your brain is about 73% water, and even mild dehydration can affect cognitive function. Just a 2% drop in hydration can lead to memory issues, difficulty focusing, and mood swings.

◎ The human nose can detect at least 1 trillion distinct scents. This ability surpasses even the most advanced artificial sensors, making your sense of smell a powerful tool for memory and survival.

◎ If uncoiled, the DNA in a single human cell would stretch about six feet long. If all the DNA in your body were laid end to end, it could reach from Earth to the Sun and back *hundreds* of times.

◎ The human body contains about 37.2 trillion cells, each performing specialized tasks to keep you alive. Despite their vast number, all of these cells originate from a single fertilized egg.

◎ Your body has more bacterial cells than human cells. The human microbiome consists of trillions of bacteria, fungi, and other microbes that play essential roles in digestion, immunity, and even mood regulation.

◎ The fastest muscles in the human body control blinking. They can contract in less than 1/100th of a second, which is why you can involuntarily shut your eyes so quickly when something gets too close.

◎ The placebo effect is so powerful that it can sometimes work even when people *know* they are taking a placebo. The brain's expectation of healing can trigger real physiological changes, from reduced pain to improved mood.

◎ Your skin is your largest organ, covering roughly 22 square feet and accounting for about 15% of your body weight. It renews itself about every 27 days, shedding millions of dead cells daily.

◎ The human body produces about a liter of mucus every day. Most of it gets swallowed without you even noticing, helping to trap dust, bacteria, and other harmful particles before they enter your lungs.

◎ When you experience a "brain freeze," it's actually your brain's way of overreacting to sudden cold exposure. The rapid temperature change in the mouth causes blood vessels in the head to constrict and then quickly expand, triggering pain.

◎ Human bones are five times stronger than steel of the same density. Despite their strength, they are also surprisingly flexible, which helps prevent fractures from everyday stress.

◎ Your blood vessels, if stretched end to end, would extend over 60,000 miles—long enough to wrap around the Earth *twice*.

◎ The human body naturally glows, emitting a faint bioluminescence. Though invisible to the naked eye, sensitive cameras have detected tiny pulses of light radiating from living cells.

◎ Dreams help process emotions, strengthen memories, and problem-solve in ways we don't fully understand. The brain is often more active during REM sleep than when you're awake.

◎ The sense of touch is so sensitive that the human finger can detect a difference in texture as small as 13 nanometers. That's roughly the size of a single strand of human DNA.

◎ Human fingernails grow about four times faster than toenails. The reason? Fingernails experience more daily wear and tear, requiring them to regenerate more quickly.

◎ The brain can rewire itself in response to new experiences, a phenomenon known as neuroplasticity. This means that learning a new skill, like playing an instrument or speaking a new language, actually reshapes brain structure.

◎ Your liver is the only organ that can completely regenerate itself. Even if up to 75% of it is removed, it can regrow to its original size within weeks.

◎ The body is capable of temporarily increasing its strength under extreme stress, a phenomenon known as hysterical strength. Cases have been reported where people lift cars or heavy objects to save others in moments of crisis.

◎ The sensation of déjà vu is still a mystery, but some theories suggest it happens when the brain mistakenly processes new information as a past memory. Others believe it may be linked to minor, unnoticed delays in brain processing.

◎ You are slightly taller in the morning than at night. Over the course of the day, gravity compresses the cartilage in your spine, reducing your height by up to half an inch.

◎ The human body emits an electric field strong enough to interfere with sensitive instruments. Some people even experience "streetlight interference," where lamps flicker or dim when they pass by—though science hasn't quite explained why.

INTERNET HISTORY

◎ The first message ever sent over the internet was "LO." In 1969, researchers at UCLA attempted to send "LOGIN" to a computer at Stanford, but the system crashed after just two letters. This marked the birth of the ARPANET, the predecessor of the modern internet.

◎ The world's first website is still online. Created by Tim Berners-Lee in 1991, the site explains how the World Wide Web works. You can visit it today at info.cern.ch, where it remains frozen in time.

◎ The first webcam was used to monitor a coffee pot. In 1991, researchers at the University of Cambridge wanted to check if coffee was available without leaving their desks, so they set up a camera streaming a grainy, black-and-white live feed of the pot. This simple invention became the ancestor of modern streaming technology.

◎ The @ symbol was almost obsolete before the internet revived it. Before email, it was primarily used in accounting and rarely appeared outside of commercial documents. Now, it's an iconic part of digital communication.

◎ Spam email predates the internet. The first known case was in 1978, when a marketer sent an unsolicited message to 393 ARPANET users advertising computer systems. Annoyed recipients complained, but the trend never stopped—billions of spam emails are sent daily.

◎ Google started as a research project called "Backrub." Larry Page and Sergey Brin's 1996 search engine analyzed backlinks to rank web pages. They later renamed it Google, inspired by "googol," a mathematical term for the number 1 followed by 100 zeros.

◎ The first item ever sold on eBay was a broken laser pointer. In 1995, eBay's founder, Pierre Omidyar, listed it as an experiment to see if people would buy items online. To his surprise, someone bought it for $14, proving that anything could be sold on the internet.

◎ Amazon started as a bookstore because books were easy to ship. Jeff Bezos believed an online store needed a large selection, and books were ideal because they didn't spoil or have size variations. Today, Amazon sells nearly everything, but its first focus was literature.

◎ The first meme on the internet dates back to 1996. The "Dancing Baby," a 3D-rendered baby doing a bizarre cha-cha, became one of the first viral sensations. It spread through email chains before social media even existed.

◎ Wikipedia's first article was about the letter "U." The site launched in 2001, and early articles were simple, sometimes just one sentence. Now, Wikipedia has over 6 million English articles and is one of the most visited websites in the world.

◎ The most disliked video in YouTube history was posted by YouTube themselves. The 2018 "YouTube Rewind" received such backlash that it quickly became the most downvoted video on the platform. YouTube eventually removed the public dislike counter—but the internet never forgets.

◎ Facebook's original name was "TheFacebook." Launched in 2004, it was initially meant for Harvard students before expanding to other universities. The "The" was dropped in 2005 after Sean Parker, co-founder of Napster, advised Mark Zuckerberg to simplify the name.

◎ The first tweet ever posted was just five words long. Twitter co-founder Jack Dorsey wrote, "just setting up my twttr" on March 21,

2006. At the time, Twitter was called "twttr," inspired by early internet naming trends.

◎ MySpace once ruled the internet. In 2006, it was the most visited website in the U.S., even surpassing Google. But after poor management decisions and the rise of Facebook, MySpace faded into digital history.

◎ The world's first mobile internet service launched in 1996. It was called i-Mode and was introduced in Japan by NTT DoCoMo. While slow by today's standards, it allowed users to check emails and browse basic web pages on flip phones long before smartphones existed.

◎ Google's homepage is so simple partly because its founders didn't know much about HTML. Larry Page and Sergey Brin preferred an uncluttered design, and since they weren't web designers, they created a minimalist search bar without distractions. The clean look became part of Google's identity.

◎ Before YouTube, a site called ShareYourWorld let users upload videos. Launched in 1997, it struggled due to slow internet speeds and storage costs. YouTube succeeded because broadband connections became faster, making video sharing practical.

◎ Netflix once offered to sell itself to Blockbuster. In 2000, Netflix approached Blockbuster about a partnership, but Blockbuster executives laughed at the idea. Today, Blockbuster has one remaining store, while Netflix dominates global streaming.

◎ The world's first banner ad had a 44% click-through rate. In 1994, AT&T ran an online ad saying, "Have you ever clicked your mouse right here?" Most users had never seen an ad before and clicked out of curiosity. Modern banner ads average less than 1% click-through.

◎ The first online purchase using a credit card was a pizza. In 1994, a customer ordered a pepperoni and mushroom pizza from Pizza Hut through its experimental online ordering system. It marked the beginning of e-commerce as we know it.

⊚ Internet Explorer was once the king of browsers. In the early 2000s, it controlled over 90% of web traffic. But slow updates and security flaws allowed competitors like Firefox and Chrome to take over, and Microsoft officially retired it in 2022.

⊚ The term "surfing the web" was coined in 1992. Librarian Jean Armour Polly used the phrase in an article about navigating the growing World Wide Web. It stuck, even though most internet users no longer think of it as "surfing."

⊚ The first .com domain name ever registered was symbolics.com in 1985. It belonged to a now-defunct computer company and is still online today as an internet history archive. By contrast, Google didn't register its domain until 1997.

⊚ The Internet Archive's Wayback Machine has saved billions of web pages. Launched in 2001, it allows users to see how websites looked decades ago. Even deleted sites and forgotten social media profiles can sometimes still be found there.

⊚ There was an entire social network before the web existed. Called **Usenet**, it launched in 1980 and allowed users to post in discussion groups. While mostly forgotten, it was the foundation for modern internet forums.

⊚ The most-visited website in the world isn't always Google. At times, TikTok has overtaken Google in traffic, showing how quickly internet habits change. The fight for digital dominance never ends.

⊚ The word "emoji" comes from Japanese. It combines "e" (picture) and "moji" (character), meaning "pictogram." Contrary to popular belief, emojis are not based on emoticons like :-) but have their own history in Japanese mobile culture.

⊚ A single email produces CO_2. Every email sent, stored, or forwarded requires energy to power servers. While tiny on an individual level, billions of emails contribute to the internet's environmental footprint.

⊚ The internet weighs about the same as a strawberry. If you calculate the weight of electrons moving through data transmissions, the entire global internet is estimated to weigh around 50 grams—less than a single fruit.

TECHNOLOGICAL TRIVIA

◎ The first robot was built in ancient Greece. Around 400 BCE, mathematician Archytas designed a wooden, steam-powered bird called "The Pigeon" that could fly short distances. It was one of history's earliest examples of automated machinery.

◎ The first alarm clock could only ring at one time. Invented by Levi Hutchins in 1787, the clock was designed to wake him up at exactly 4 a.m. every day. He never thought to make it adjustable because, to him, 4 a.m. was the only time worth waking up.

◎ The Apollo 11 lunar module had less computing power than a modern smartphone. The onboard computer had only 64 KB of memory and processed instructions slower than an early Nintendo console. Despite this, it successfully guided humans to the Moon and back.

◎ The world's first vending machine dispensed holy water. Invented by Greek engineer Hero of Alexandria in the 1st century CE, it used a system of levers and weights to release a measured amount of water when a coin was inserted. It was designed to prevent temple visitors from taking more than their fair share.

◎ The first television broadcast was just a simple line. In 1928, inventor John Logie Baird demonstrated an early TV transmission using a single moving white line. It wasn't much to look at, but it paved the way for modern television.

◉ Early cars had no gas pedals. Instead, they were controlled with a lever, similar to a boat throttle. The modern pedal layout—accelerator, brake, and clutch—wasn't standardized until the 1908 Ford Model T.

◉ The first recorded use of a robotic arm was in 1961. General Motors installed the Unimate, a robotic arm, on an assembly line to automate car manufacturing. It weighed over 2,700 pounds and could precisely handle molten metal.

◉ The typewriter was originally designed to help the blind. In 1808, Italian inventor Pellegrino Turri built an early typewriter so his blind friend could write letters more easily. The first commercially successful typewriter wouldn't appear until 1873.

◉ Some traffic lights can sense when you're looking at them. Using infrared sensors and AI, modern traffic systems in cities like Sydney can detect driver behavior and adjust light cycles accordingly. This helps improve traffic flow and reduce wait times.

◉ The first telephone book only had 50 names. Published in 1878 in New Haven, Connecticut, the book listed only a handful of businesses and residents. There were no phone numbers—just names, since operators connected all calls manually.

◉ The world's smallest camera is smaller than a grain of salt. Developed for medical use, it measures just 0.65 mm across and can be inserted into the body for high-resolution imaging. It's so tiny that it's disposable after one use.

◉ The floppy disk was once considered cutting-edge storage. When introduced in the 1970s, an 8-inch floppy disk could store about 80 KB of data. That's not even enough for a single modern smartphone photo.

◉ The first commercial airplane flight lasted only 23 minutes. In 1914, a small biplane carried one passenger across Tampa Bay, Florida. The fare was $400 (adjusted for inflation), making it one of the most expensive short flights in history.

⊚ The original fax machine was invented before the telephone. Scottish inventor Alexander Bain developed a primitive version in 1843, using a pendulum and electrical signals to transmit images. However, it didn't become practical until the 20th century.

⊚ The world's first 3D-printed car was built in just 44 hours. Created in 2014 by Local Motors, the *Strati* was made almost entirely of 3D-printed parts, except for the battery and tires. It was fully functional and could reach speeds of 40 mph.

⊚ The first self-driving car was developed in the 1980s. Named "Navlab," it was a van outfitted with cameras and sensors by Carnegie Mellon University. It could drive itself at speeds up to 20 mph—a fraction of today's autonomous car speeds.

⊚ The compact disc (CD) was designed to hold Beethoven's Ninth Symphony. Engineers at Philips and Sony decided that a CD should store at least 74 minutes of audio to fit the full symphony. This set the standard for digital music storage.

⊚ The wristwatch was originally invented for women. In the early 1800s, wristwatches were considered jewelry, while men preferred pocket watches. That changed during World War I when soldiers found wristwatches more practical in battle.

⊚ The first recorded use of a prosthetic limb dates back to ancient Egypt. Archaeologists discovered a wooden toe on a 3,000-year-old mummy, designed to help the wearer walk normally. It was surprisingly well-crafted, even by modern standards.

⊚ The Hubble Space Telescope is constantly moving at 17,500 mph. Even while capturing breathtaking images of the universe, it orbits Earth at speeds that would allow it to travel from New York to Los Angeles in under 12 minutes.

⊚ The first electric car was built in 1884. British inventor Thomas Parker created an early battery-powered vehicle decades before gasoline cars took over. Electric cars actually outsold gasoline models in the early 1900s before fading into obscurity.

◎ The first parachute jump happened before airplanes existed. In 1797, André-Jacques Garnerin jumped from a hot air balloon using a silk parachute. His landing was rough, but he survived, proving that controlled parachute descents were possible.

◎ The International Space Station is the most expensive structure ever built. With a total cost exceeding $150 billion, it's more expensive than all the world's tallest buildings combined. It's also the only structure that requires a spaceship to visit.

◎ The first ATM was tested using a fake check from a candy machine. When engineer John Shepherd-Barron invented the automated teller machine in 1967, he used a gum-dispensing mechanism to test whether it could properly process transactions.

◎ The first artificial heart kept a patient alive for 112 days. In 1982, Dr. Barney Clark became the first person to receive a permanent artificial heart. It wasn't perfect—he had to remain hooked up to a machine—but it paved the way for modern heart implants.

◎ The world's largest battery can power 1.3 million homes for an hour. Located in California, this massive lithium-ion battery storage facility stabilizes the energy grid. It holds enough power to light up a small city during peak demand.

◎ A tiny computer once traveled inside a butterfly. Scientists attached a miniature tracking device to a monarch butterfly's back, weighing less than a raindrop. This helped researchers understand its 3,000-mile migration journey.

SPACE EXPLORATION

◎ The first human-made object to reach space was a German V-2 rocket in 1944. It wasn't an exploration mission—scientists were testing missile technology during World War II. After the war, the U.S. and Soviet Union took the technology to develop their own space programs.

◎ The Soviet Union launched *Sputnik 1* in 1957, the first artificial satellite to orbit Earth. It was a simple metal sphere with four antennas, yet its beeping signal terrified Americans, leading to the creation of NASA and the start of the Space Race.

◎ Yuri Gagarin became the first human in space in 1961, but he almost didn't survive re-entry. His *Vostok 1* capsule had no soft-landing system, so he had to eject and parachute down separately—an event the Soviet Union kept secret for years.

◎ The Apollo 11 crew left behind more than just footprints on the Moon. They left a plaque, an American flag, and even a collection of scientific instruments. They also abandoned the lunar module's ascent stage, which eventually crashed back onto the Moon.

◎ The famous "Earthrise" photo, taken by Apollo 8 in 1968, changed humanity's view of the planet. Seeing Earth as a tiny, fragile sphere in the vastness of space helped inspire the modern environmental movement.

◎ Valentina Tereshkova became the first woman in space in 1963, beating American women to space by 20 years. She completed 48 orbits aboard *Vostok 6*, but suffered nausea and extreme discomfort in her poorly designed suit.

◎ *Voyager 1*, launched in 1977, is now the farthest human-made object from Earth, over 14 billion miles away. It carries a "Golden Record" with sounds and images from Earth, just in case an alien civilization ever finds it.

◎ Apollo 12 astronauts nearly lost their Moon landing when lightning struck their spacecraft moments after launch. The entire guidance system went down, but quick thinking from mission control saved the mission—using an obscure reset switch known to just one engineer.

◎ The Mars rover *Opportunity* was originally designed to last just 90 days but ended up surviving nearly 15 years. It traveled 28 miles across Mars' surface before a massive dust storm finally silenced it in 2018. Its final message to NASA? "My battery is low and it's getting dark."

◎ The Space Shuttle program ran for 30 years, from 1981 to 2011, and was the first reusable spacecraft system. While it enabled incredible missions, two tragedies—the *Challenger* explosion in 1986 and the *Columbia* disaster in 2003—ultimately led to its retirement.

◎ The first spacewalk in history, performed by Alexei Leonov in 1965, nearly ended in disaster. His suit inflated so much in the vacuum of space that he struggled to get back inside his capsule, forcing him to vent oxygen until he could barely breathe.

◎ Neil Armstrong and Buzz Aldrin almost didn't make it off the Moon. A broken circuit in their lunar module threatened to leave them stranded, but Aldrin improvised by jamming a felt-tip pen into the switch—saving their lives.

◎ The International Space Station orbits Earth at 17,500 mph, completing one full orbit every 90 minutes. This means astronauts experience 16 sunrises and 16 sunsets every single day.

◎ The first living creature to orbit Earth was a stray dog named Laika, launched by the Soviet Union in 1957. She had no way to return and perished within hours due to overheating, making her a tragic pioneer of space exploration.

◎ In 2019, China's *Chang'e 4* mission became the first to land on the far side of the Moon. Because radio signals couldn't reach that side, China had to place a relay satellite in orbit just to communicate with the lander.

◎ The first private spacecraft to reach orbit was SpaceX's *Falcon 1* in 2008. This paved the way for commercial spaceflight, leading to the first privately-funded crewed missions to the ISS over a decade later.

◎ NASA once misplaced a bag of Moon dust collected during Apollo 11. It was later found in a private collection and, after a legal battle, sold at auction for $1.8 million.

◎ The Saturn V rocket remains the most powerful rocket ever built. It stood 363 feet tall, burned 20 tons of fuel per second, and could generate more thrust than 85 Hoover Dams.

◎ The Hubble Space Telescope was launched in 1990, but its mirror was flawed, causing blurry images. NASA had to send astronauts to install corrective optics in space—essentially giving Hubble a giant pair of glasses.

◎ In 1971, Apollo 15 astronauts left a small aluminum statue called *Fallen Astronaut* on the Moon. It was placed as a memorial to honor all astronauts and cosmonauts who had died in the pursuit of space exploration.

◎ The first spacecraft to visit another planet was *Mariner 2*, which flew past Venus in 1962. It confirmed Venus' blistering temperatures, proving the planet was nothing like Earth despite its similar size.

◎ Spacecraft don't technically experience "zero gravity." Instead, they are in a constant state of free fall, giving astronauts the sensation of weightlessness as they orbit Earth.

◎ NASA's *Perseverance* rover on Mars has a tiny helicopter named *Ingenuity*. It became the first aircraft to achieve powered flight on another planet, proving that flying is possible in Mars' thin atmosphere.

◎ The *Genesis* probe collected particles from the Sun, but its parachute failed during reentry in 2001, causing it to crash-land in Utah. Amazingly, scientists were still able to recover some solar wind samples from the wreckage.

◎ The Apollo 14 astronauts played golf on the Moon. Alan Shepard used a makeshift club to hit two golf balls, one of which traveled an estimated 2,400 feet due to the Moon's lower gravity.

◎ NASA once considered sending a floating probe to explore the methane lakes of Saturn's moon Titan. The *Titan Mare Explorer* was never funded, but future missions might still explore Titan's frigid, alien seas.

◎ The *New Horizons* spacecraft, which flew past Pluto in 2015, is now exploring the distant Kuiper Belt. It will continue sending data back to Earth until at least the 2040s.

◎ The Soviet Union planned to send cosmonauts to the Moon, but their massive N1 rocket exploded four times during tests. Each explosion was so powerful that it destroyed the launch pad, ending their lunar ambitions.

◎ In 1965, *Gemini 6* and *Gemini 7* performed the first space rendezvous, coming within a foot of each other in orbit. The astronauts exchanged jokes over the radio, with one crew pretending to report a "UFO" sighting—Santa Claus.

◎ The Sun accounts for 99.8% of the total mass in our solar system. If it were the size of a basketball, Earth would be about the size of a sesame seed.

◎ There's a massive hexagon-shaped storm on Saturn's north pole. It's been swirling for decades and is large enough to fit four Earths inside it.

◎ A single day on Mercury lasts longer than its entire year. Because of its slow rotation and fast orbit, the Sun rises only once every 176 Earth days.

◎ If you could stand on the surface of Venus, you'd be crushed by atmospheric pressure equivalent to being 3,000 feet underwater. Add in 860°F temperatures and acid rain, and it's one of the worst places to visit.

◎ The largest volcano in the solar system, Olympus Mons, is on Mars. It's nearly three times the height of Mount Everest and so wide that you wouldn't even notice you were standing on a mountain.

◎ Jupiter's moon Europa has an ocean beneath its icy crust that contains more liquid water than all of Earth's oceans combined. Scientists believe it may be one of the best places to search for extraterrestrial life.

◎ Space isn't completely silent. Although sound waves can't travel through a vacuum, radio waves emitted by planets and stars can be converted into eerie, otherworldly sounds.

◎ Pluto was demoted from planet status in 2006, but it still has five moons, an atmosphere, and active ice volcanoes. Some scientists continue to argue that it should be reclassified as a planet.

◎ The Hubble Space Telescope can see galaxies over 13 billion light-years away. That means it's looking so far into the past that it captures images of the universe as it was just a few hundred million years after the Big Bang.

◎ There's a giant cloud of alcohol floating in space near the center of the Milky Way. Unfortunately, it's mostly methanol, making it undrinkable for space travelers.

◎ If two pieces of the same metal touch in space, they fuse together permanently. This process, called cold welding, doesn't happen on Earth because of oxidation in our atmosphere.

◎ Saturn's rings aren't solid but made up of countless ice and rock particles, some as tiny as dust and others as large as houses. Despite their size, the rings are incredibly thin—only about 30 feet thick in some areas.

◎ Neutron stars are so dense that a sugar-cube-sized piece of one would weigh as much as Mount Everest. They spin at incredible speeds, with some rotating hundreds of times per second.

◎ Uranus is the only planet that rotates on its side. Scientists believe it was knocked over by a massive collision billions of years ago.

◎ The planets in our solar system are practically next door compared to the stars. While Voyager 2 reached Neptune in 12 years, the closest star, Proxima Centauri, is over 10,000 times farther away. Even at the speed of our fastest spacecraft, it would take 17,000 years to get there!

◎ The largest-known asteroid in the solar system, Ceres, is so big that it was reclassified as a dwarf planet. It even has its own atmosphere and signs of ancient water.

◎ The coldest place in the universe ever recorded is a nebula known as the Boomerang Nebula. At -457.7°F, it's just a fraction of a degree above absolute zero.

◎ The Sun's core is so hot that a piece the size of a sugar cube would produce more energy than a nuclear bomb. It takes light from the core about 100,000 years to reach the surface before heading toward Earth.

◎ The Andromeda Galaxy is on a collision course with the Milky Way. In about 4.5 billion years, the two galaxies will merge, creating a new, larger galaxy.

◎ Black holes don't actually "suck" things in. Instead, they warp space-time so severely that anything crossing the event horizon can never escape.

◎ A day on Mars is only about 40 minutes longer than a day on Earth. Because of this, NASA scientists working on Mars missions sometimes adjust their schedules to "Mars time," gradually shifting their sleep cycles.

◎ Some exoplanets, known as hot Jupiters, orbit their stars in just a few days. These massive gas giants are often closer to their stars than Mercury is to the Sun.

◎ The largest canyon in the solar system, Valles Marineris, is on Mars. It's over 2,500 miles long—roughly the width of the entire United States.

◎ Astronauts in space grow up to two inches taller due to the lack of gravity compressing their spines. Unfortunately, they shrink back to normal once they return to Earth.

◎ A starquake, caused by sudden shifts in neutron stars, can release more energy in seconds than the Sun emits in 100,000 years. These extreme events are some of the most powerful in the universe.

◎ The first living creature to orbit Earth was a dog named Laika in 1957. She rode aboard the Soviet satellite Sputnik 2, paving the way for human spaceflight.

◎ The Kuiper Belt, home to Pluto and other icy bodies, is a massive region beyond Neptune. It's believed to contain trillions of objects, including some that could be larger than Pluto.

◎ The James Webb Space Telescope can detect infrared light from galaxies billions of light-years away. This allows it to peer further into the universe's past than any telescope before it.

◎ If you fell into a black hole, you'd experience "spaghettification" due to extreme gravitational forces stretching you into a thin strand. Fortunately, you'd be obliterated long before reaching the singularity.

THE PLANETS

◎ Mercury has the most extreme temperature swings of any planet in the solar system. Because it has no atmosphere to trap heat, daytime temperatures soar to 800°F, while nighttime temperatures plunge to -290°F.

◎ Venus is the hottest planet, even though Mercury is closer to the Sun. Its thick carbon dioxide atmosphere creates a runaway greenhouse effect, trapping heat and keeping surface temperatures around 860°F—hot enough to melt lead.

◎ A day on Venus lasts longer than its year. Venus takes 243 Earth days to rotate once on its axis but only 225 Earth days to complete an orbit around the Sun.

◎ Earth is the only known planet where fire can burn naturally. Without oxygen in the atmosphere, fire wouldn't ignite on any other planet in our solar system.

◎ Mars has the tallest volcano in the solar system. Olympus Mons is about 13.6 miles (22 km) high—nearly three times the height of Mount Everest—and it covers an area roughly the size of Arizona.

⊚ The dust storms on Mars can last for months and sometimes engulf the entire planet. These storms are so intense that they can block out the Sun, causing dramatic temperature drops.

⊚ Jupiter has a storm called the Great Red Spot that has been raging for at least 350 years. This massive storm is twice the size of Earth and has winds reaching up to 400 mph.

⊚ A year on Jupiter is nearly 12 Earth years long, but a day lasts only 9 hours and 56 minutes. This means Jupiter rotates so fast that it bulges at the equator, making it more oblate than spherical.

⊚ Saturn's rings are made mostly of ice and rock, with some pieces as small as grains of sand and others as big as mountains. The rings are also surprisingly thin—only about 30 feet thick in some places.

⊚ If you could find a bathtub big enough, Saturn would float in water. Its density is lower than water, making it the only planet in our solar system that would be buoyant.

⊚ Uranus rotates on its side, tilted at an extreme angle of 98 degrees. This bizarre tilt likely resulted from a massive collision with an Earth-sized object billions of years ago.

⊚ A year on Uranus lasts 84 Earth years. Because of its extreme axial tilt, each of its poles experiences 42 years of continuous sunlight followed by 42 years of darkness.

⊚ Neptune is the windiest planet in the solar system. Its winds can reach speeds of over 1,200 mph—faster than the speed of sound on Earth.

⊚ Neptune's Great Dark Spot was a massive storm similar to Jupiter's Great Red Spot, but it mysteriously disappeared in the 1990s. Scientists believe it may have dissipated and reformed elsewhere.

⊚ Pluto was once considered the ninth planet but was reclassified as a dwarf planet in 2006. Despite this, many planetary scientists still debate whether it should be reinstated as a full-fledged planet.

◎ The largest moon in the solar system is Ganymede, which orbits Jupiter. It's even bigger than Mercury and has a magnetic field—something no other moon possesses.

◎ Titan, Saturn's largest moon, has lakes and rivers of liquid methane and ethane. Its thick atmosphere makes it the only moon in the solar system with weather and a hydrological cycle similar to Earth's—but with methane instead of water.

◎ The Sun's gravity is so strong that it controls the orbits of planets billions of miles away. Even distant Pluto, which orbits at an average of 3.7 billion miles from the Sun, is still locked in its gravitational grip.

◎ The asteroid belt between Mars and Jupiter isn't as densely packed as movies suggest. A spacecraft traveling through it has a very low chance of colliding with an asteroid because the objects are spread out over vast distances.

◎ The Kuiper Belt, a region beyond Neptune, is home to icy bodies and dwarf planets, including Pluto. It's like a second asteroid belt but made mostly of frozen water, methane, and ammonia.

◎ The coldest place in the solar system is on the moon Triton, which orbits Neptune. Temperatures there drop as low as -391°F, making it even colder than Pluto.

◎ Venus and Uranus are the only two planets that rotate in the opposite direction of most planets in the solar system. This means that on Venus, the Sun rises in the west and sets in the east.

◎ Jupiter has 95 known moons, the most of any planet. Scientists continue discovering more, making Jupiter's moon count higher than that of any other planet in the solar system.

◎ Earth is the only planet where water exists in all three states—solid, liquid, and gas—at the same time. This is thanks to its unique atmospheric pressure and temperature range.

◎ Mars once had a thicker atmosphere and flowing rivers. Billions of years ago, its climate was more Earth-like, but solar winds stripped away much of its atmosphere, turning it into the cold, dry planet we see today.

◎ The surface of Mercury is covered in wrinkles called "lobate scarps," formed as the planet's core cooled and contracted over time. Some of these cliffs are hundreds of miles long and rise thousands of feet high.

◎ Uranus has a faint set of rings, though they are much darker and less visible than Saturn's. These rings are made of large chunks of rock, making them almost invisible in normal light.

◎ Triton is one of the coldest places in the solar system, with temperatures reaching -391°F, rivaling Pluto. However, the coldest recorded temperatures in the solar system are found in permanently shadowed craters at the Moon's south pole, reaching -410°F.

WEIRD HOLLYWOOD

◎ The Hollywood sign used to say "Hollywoodland." Originally built in 1923 as a real estate advertisement, the sign was meant to last only 18 months. It wasn't until 1949 that the "land" was removed, leaving behind the iconic landmark we know today.

◎ The first Oscar winners were announced before the ceremony. In 1929, the winners were revealed to the press three months in advance. After newspapers spoiled the results, the Academy switched to sealed envelopes, creating the tradition of suspenseful award announcements.

◎ Charlie Chaplin once lost a Charlie Chaplin look-alike contest. Legend has it that he entered under a fake name, but the judges didn't recognize him. He didn't even make it to the finals.

◎ The Hollywood Walk of Fame has a typo. Julia Louis-Dreyfus' star originally misspelled her name as "Luis Dreyfus." She took it in stride, joking that she was honored they even considered her.

◎ MGM's iconic lion once escaped its cage. In the 1920s, the original lion used in the studio's famous logo roamed the streets of Hollywood after breaking free. It was eventually captured unharmed, but not before giving a few pedestrians the fright of their lives.

⊚ The Wizard of Oz's Tin Man makeup was so toxic it hospitalized the actor. The original Tin Man, Buddy Ebsen, suffered severe lung poisoning from aluminum dust in the makeup. He had to be replaced, and his scenes were reshot—but his cough lasted for years.

⊚ A chimpanzee was once given a Golden Globe. In 1951, the Hollywood Foreign Press Association awarded a special honorary Golden Globe to J. Fred Muggs, a chimp who co-hosted NBC's *Today* show. Somehow, he never got around to giving an acceptance speech.

⊚ A real skeleton was used in *Poltergeist.* The skeletons floating in the pool scene weren't props—they were actual human remains, as real bones were cheaper than plastic ones at the time. Crew members later claimed the film was cursed.

⊚ A James Bond actor was actually a spy. Before becoming a Bond villain, Christopher Lee worked for British intelligence in World War II. He was so secretive about his past that he once corrected *Lord of the Rings* director Peter Jackson on what a real stabbing sounds like.

⊚ A movie was once filmed in a real haunted house. *The Amityville Horror* (1979) shot scenes in a house so eerie that actors reported strange noises, moving objects, and an unexplained sense of dread. Some refused to stay on set overnight.

⊚ Alfred Hitchcock, notorious for his elaborate pranks, once pranked his cast with a meal that made them sick. While filming *The 39 Steps*, Hitchcock fed his actors a dinner laced with a strong laxative—just to see how they'd react. No one found it as funny as he did.

⊚ *The Exorcist* set was exorcised. After multiple accidents—including a fire that destroyed most of the set—the production hired a priest to perform an actual exorcism. The chaos didn't stop, but the film became one of the most infamous horror movies ever made.

⊚ There's a time capsule under the Hollywood Walk of Fame. Buried in 1994, it contains letters from celebrities, a script from *Casablanca*, and a pair of Betty White's shoes. It won't be opened until 2044.

◎ A dog has a star on the Hollywood Walk of Fame. Lassie, the famous collie, was honored with her own star in 1960. Technically, she's one of the few stars who never had a scandal.

◎ Arnold Schwarzenegger wasn't allowed to dub himself. When *The Terminator* was released in Germany, producers hired a different actor for the German dub. They thought Arnold's Austrian accent sounded too "rural" for the futuristic cyborg assassin.

◎ A stunt double once played twins in a movie. In *The Parent Trap* (1961), Hayley Mills' twin was often played by her body double. But in one scene, her double's face was accidentally visible, leading to a Hollywood editing blunder.

◎ In *Seinfeld's The Apology* (Season 9, Episode 9), Jerry's girlfriend casually walks around topless—just out of frame in the original 4:3 version. But when the show was remastered in 16:9, the expanded frame accidentally revealed her bare breast, surprising fans and editors alike.

◎ Marlon Brando once wore a bucket on his head in a movie. Frustrated with the direction of *The Island of Dr. Moreau* (1996), Brando insisted on wearing a metal bucket as a hat in several scenes. No one dared to tell him no.

◎ The original *Jurassic Park* T. rex kept malfunctioning. The animatronic dinosaur would randomly start moving, even when turned off, terrifying the crew. Filming during rainstorms made it even worse, as the water would cause it to glitch and lunge unexpectedly.

◎ Walt Disney's last words remain a mystery. On his deathbed, he wrote "Kurt Russell" on a piece of paper, and no one knows why. The actor was a Disney contract player at the time but had no idea what Disney meant by it.

◎ *Psycho* was the first film to show a toilet flushing. Before Hitchcock's 1960 thriller, Hollywood's production codes forbade showing toilets being used. The flushing scene in *Psycho* was oddly controversial at the time.

⊚ The *Titanic* cast was poisoned. During filming, cast and crew were mysteriously drugged with PCP-laced chowder, causing hallucinations and sickness. To this day, no one knows who spiked the food.

⊚ Hogan's Heroes star Bob Crane was murdered in 1978 under mysterious circumstances. His friend John Carpenter (not the director) was a suspect, but theories that Crane faked his own death remain purely speculative.

⊚ The *E.T.* puppet cost more than a house. The animatronic E.T. used in the 1982 film was so complex that it cost over $1 million to build—more than the average home at the time. It required multiple puppeteers just to operate its face.

⊚ A director once refused to say "Cut!" out of superstition. John Ford, one of Hollywood's most legendary directors, believed that yelling "Cut!" would jinx a scene. Instead, he'd just mutter, "That's enough of that."

⊚ There's a secret apartment inside Disneyland. Walt Disney had a hidden apartment above the firehouse on Main Street, where he would sometimes stay overnight. Today, a single lamp in the window stays lit in his memory.

⊚ Keanu Reeves secretly funded *The Matrix* crew's bonuses. After the massive success of *The Matrix*, Reeves gave much of his earnings to the film's costume and effects teams, believing they deserved more for their hard work.

⊚ An Oscar once disappeared for 12 years. In 2000, a shipment of 55 Oscar statuettes was stolen. Most were recovered in a dumpster a week later, but one remained missing until 2012 when it mysteriously resurfaced at a flea market.

⊚ There's a film that has been playing continuously since 1975. *The Rocky Horror Picture Show* holds the record for the longest-running theatrical release. Midnight screenings with audience participation have kept it alive for nearly 50 years.

POPULAR MOVIES

◎ *Jaws* (1975) had so many problems with its mechanical shark that director Steven Spielberg resorted to hiding it for most of the film. This unintentional change made the movie scarier, as audiences were left to imagine the monster lurking beneath the water.

◎ *The Wizard of Oz* (1939) used a toxic substance for the Wicked Witch's green makeup—copper-based paint that burned actress Margaret Hamilton's skin. After suffering severe burns from an on-set accident, she refused to work with fire effects again.

◎ In *Star Wars: A New Hope* (1977), the famous sound of a lightsaber was created by blending the hum of an old movie projector with the buzz of a television set's back panel. The effect was discovered accidentally when a sound designer walked past a TV with a microphone.

◎ *Titanic* (1997) was so cold during filming that many extras suffered from hypothermia. Kate Winslet refused to wear a wetsuit for her water scenes, leading to a bout of pneumonia.

◎ The "Here's Johnny!" scene in *The Shining* (1980) was improvised by Jack Nicholson. Director Stanley Kubrick, who was unaware of the famous Johnny Carson reference, nearly cut it from the film.

⊚ The alien language in *Avatar* (2009) wasn't just gibberish—it was a fully constructed language created by a linguist, complete with grammar and vocabulary. Some fans have even learned to speak it fluently.

⊚ The famous boulder chase in *Raiders of the Lost Ark* (1981) featured a real, 300-pound fiberglass boulder rolling toward Harrison Ford. He performed the stunt himself and barely outran it in multiple takes.

⊚ *Pulp Fiction* (1994) revitalized John Travolta's career, but he was far from the first choice for Vincent Vega. Quentin Tarantino originally wanted Michael Madsen, but when he turned it down, Travolta got the part for a fraction of his usual salary.

⊚ In *The Godfather* (1972), the cat in Marlon Brando's lap wasn't in the script. It wandered onto the set, and Brando picked it up, unintentionally adding to his character's quiet menace.

⊚ *The Dark Knight* (2008) features one of the most famous improvised moments in film history. Heath Ledger's Joker slow-clapping in his jail cell wasn't scripted but became one of the most chilling moments in the film.

⊚ *Jurassic Park* (1993) changed the way movies used CGI, but the dinosaurs were originally supposed to be stop-motion. After seeing a CGI test of a T-Rex running, Spielberg scrapped the stop-motion plan and went digital.

⊚ The DeLorean in *Back to the Future* (1985) was originally supposed to be a time-traveling refrigerator. The idea was changed because filmmakers worried kids might trap themselves in real refrigerators while trying to time travel.

⊚ *Casablanca* (1942) was filmed before the script was finished, forcing actors to improvise many scenes. Ingrid Bergman reportedly didn't know until the final days of filming whether her character would stay with Rick or leave with Laszlo.

⊚ *E.T. the Extra-Terrestrial* (1982) used Reese's Pieces as a key plot device only because M&M's refused to be featured. After the movie's release, Reese's Pieces sales skyrocketed by over 65%.

◎ The mask worn by Michael Myers in *Halloween* (1978) was a cheap, modified Captain Kirk mask bought for under $2. The production crew widened the eyes and painted it white, creating one of the most terrifying horror movie icons.

◎ The famous "I'm the king of the world!" line in *Titanic* (1997) was completely improvised by Leonardo DiCaprio. James Cameron loved it so much that he kept it in the final cut.

◎ *The Silence of the Lambs* (1991) was the first horror film to win Best Picture at the Oscars. Anthony Hopkins, despite being the film's lead, had only 16 minutes of screen time as Hannibal Lecter.

◎ *Forrest Gump* (1994) featured real historical footage, but Tom Hanks' character was inserted using groundbreaking visual effects. The team painstakingly altered old clips to make it look like Forrest was shaking hands with U.S. presidents.

◎ In *Inception* (2010), the spinning top at the end leaves audiences questioning reality, but Christopher Nolan has refused to reveal the answer. Even Michael Caine, who appears in the film, once asked Nolan about it, only to be told, "If you're in the scene, it's reality."

◎ *The Matrix* (1999) popularized "bullet time," a visual effect that made slow-motion action sequences appear groundbreaking. The technique involved actors moving at normal speed while dozens of cameras captured the scene from multiple angles.

◎ *Gladiator* (2000) had to use CGI to complete Oliver Reed's scenes after he died during filming. The digital effects team reconstructed his face using existing footage to finish his performance.

◎ *Schindler's List* (1993) was mostly shot in black and white, but one girl's red coat was left in color as a symbol of innocence. That same girl is later seen in a pile of corpses, marking one of the film's most heartbreaking moments.

◎ The budget for *Mad Max: Fury Road* (2015) ballooned due to its practical stunts, but nearly everything seen on screen is real. The giant pole-swinging warriors were actual stunt performers doing their own dangerous acrobatics.

◎ *Goodfellas* (1990) features an unscripted moment where Joe Pesci's "Funny how?" line was improvised. The tension in the scene was real, as none of the other actors knew what was coming.

◎ *Rocky* (1976) was shot on a shoestring budget, so the famous run up the Philadelphia Art Museum steps was done with a single camera and a borrowed van. Sylvester Stallone didn't even have permits to film in most locations.

◎ The chestburster scene in *Alien* (1979) was so shocking that the actors' reactions were real. The cast wasn't told exactly what would happen, leading to their genuine horror when the creature erupted from John Hurt's chest.

◎ In *Fight Club* (1999), there's a Starbucks cup visible in nearly every scene. Director David Fincher included them as a subtle joke about corporate culture.

◎ *The Lord of the Rings: The Fellowship of the Ring* (2001) features a moment where Viggo Mortensen kicks a helmet and screams. His agony was real—he had actually broken his toe during the take.

◎ *Interstellar* (2014) used real scientific calculations to create its depiction of a black hole. Astrophysicists later confirmed that the film's black hole, Gargantua, was one of the most realistic ever seen on screen.

◎ The Wizard of Oz (1939) was filmed in both sepia-tone and Technicolor, but the iconic ruby slippers were originally silver in L. Frank Baum's book. They were changed to red to take full advantage of the dazzling new color process.

◎ The shower scene in Psycho (1960) contains 78 camera cuts and lasts just 45 seconds, yet it took seven days to film. The "blood" swirling down the drain was actually chocolate syrup, chosen because it looked more realistic in black and white.

◎ Gone with the Wind (1939) was the first movie to use the word "damn" in its dialogue. Producer David O. Selznick paid a fine of $5,000 to keep Rhett Butler's famous line: "Frankly, my dear, I don't give a damn."

◎ The original Godzilla (1954) was inspired by the atomic bombings of Hiroshima and Nagasaki, serving as an allegory for nuclear destruction. The monster's skin texture was modeled after keloid scars found on radiation victims.

◎ In Casablanca (1942), Humphrey Bogart had to stand on boxes in some scenes because Ingrid Bergman was two inches taller than him. The movie's famous final line, "Here's looking at you, kid," was an unscripted ad-lib.

◎ Walt Disney's Snow White and the Seven Dwarfs (1937) was the first full-length animated feature and was considered a huge financial risk. The film was so groundbreaking that Disney had to invent new animation techniques, including a multi-plane camera for depth.

◎ James Dean only starred in three films—Rebel Without a Cause (1955), East of Eden (1955), and Giant (1956)—before his tragic death at 24. Despite his brief career, he remains one of Hollywood's most iconic figures.

◎ Alfred Hitchcock's The Birds (1963) used live birds for many attack scenes, but some were mechanical. Tippi Hedren was genuinely injured during filming when live birds were tied to her costume and flung at her.

◎ Charlie Chaplin's The Great Dictator (1940) was a bold satire of Adolf Hitler at a time when the U.S. had not yet entered World War II. Chaplin later said he would never have made the film had he known the full extent of the Holocaust.

◎ Singing in the Rain (1952) was filmed using milk mixed with water to make the raindrops more visible on camera. Gene Kelly performed the title song and dance number while running a fever of 103°F.

◎ Orson Welles' Citizen Kane (1941) revolutionized filmmaking with deep-focus cinematography and non-linear storytelling. The mysterious "Rosebud" sled was one of three props made for the film—two were burned, and the last one sold at auction for over $200,000.

◎ Audrey Hepburn's iconic black dress in Breakfast at Tiffany's (1961) was designed by Hubert de Givenchy. One of the original dresses from the film was auctioned for nearly $1 million in 2006.

◎ Bela Lugosi, famous for his role as Dracula (1931), was so typecast that he was buried in his vampire cape at his request. Despite his iconic status, he died nearly penniless due to a lack of roles in his later years.

◎ Marlon Brando famously mumbled his way through On the Waterfront (1954), forcing co-stars to strain to hear him. His method acting helped define a new, more naturalistic style of film performance.

◎ The original King Kong (1933) used stop-motion animation and miniature sets to bring the giant ape to life. The film was so popular that some theaters played it continuously for weeks to sold-out audiences.

◎ Shirley Temple, the biggest child star of the 1930s, was once given a full-sized Oscar at age six. The Academy later introduced a special "Juvenile Oscar" category because of her success.

◎ The Seven Year Itch (1955) features Marilyn Monroe's iconic subway dress scene, which became one of the most famous images in cinema history. The gust of wind was created using an industrial fan, and the scene had to be reshot multiple times due to noise from the crowd.

◎ Dr. Strangelove (1964) was originally filmed with a serious ending, but Stanley Kubrick changed it to a dark comedy. Peter Sellers played three roles in the film, improvising much of his dialogue, including the moment where he accidentally calls the U.S. president "Mein Führer."

◎ The Magnificent Seven (1960) was a Western remake of Akira Kurosawa's Seven Samurai (1954), replacing swords with guns. The film's iconic theme song later became the jingle for Marlboro cigarettes.

◎ James Bond's Aston Martin DB5 from Goldfinger (1964) became so iconic that it was later used in multiple Bond films. The car, equipped with machine guns and ejector seats, set the standard for spy gadgets in cinema.

⊚ The Sound of Music (1965) became the highest-grossing film of its time, but Christopher Plummer, who played Captain Von Trapp, called it "The Sound of Mucus" and disliked the experience of making it.

⊚ The Ten Commandments (1956) had one of the most expensive special effects of its era: the parting of the Red Sea. The effect was achieved by filming water being poured into a tank and then playing the footage in reverse.

⊚ Some Like It Hot (1959) was so controversial for its cross-dressing storyline that it was released without the usual Hollywood Production Code seal. It became one of the funniest films of all time and helped bring about a shift toward more relaxed film censorship.

⊚ Alfred Hitchcock's Vertigo (1958) was a box office disappointment upon release but is now considered one of the greatest films ever made. Its hypnotic use of color and camera work created a sense of disorientation that matched the film's themes of obsession.

⊚ The original Planet of the Apes (1968) featured a shocking twist ending that wasn't in the original novel. The ruined Statue of Liberty was suggested by Rod Serling, creator of The Twilight Zone, and became one of the most famous twist endings in film history.

⊚ Bette Davis almost turned down All About Eve (1950) until she realized it would be one of the best roles of her career. Her famous line, "Fasten your seatbelts, it's going to be a bumpy night," became an instant classic.

⊚ The Third Man (1949) has one of the greatest movie themes ever, played entirely on a zither. The haunting tune became so popular that it topped music charts in multiple countries.

⊚ Laurel and Hardy's Way Out West (1937) features a famous soft-shoe dance that became one of their most beloved routines. The duo often performed it for fun at Hollywood parties.

⊚ Cleopatra (1963) nearly bankrupted 20th Century Fox due to its massive budget. Elizabeth Taylor's 65 costume changes set a record for the most in a single film, with one dress alone costing over $200,000.

⊚ The number 13 is feared in many cultures, with some buildings skipping the 13th floor entirely. However, in Italy, 13 is actually considered lucky, while 17 is the number to avoid.

⊚ If you shuffle a standard deck of 52 cards, there's an almost 100% chance that no one in history has ever shuffled it into that exact order before. The number of possible arrangements is a staggering 8.06×10^{67}.

⊚ The number 9 has a special trick in multiplication. Any number multiplied by 9 will have digits that sum to 9 (e.g., 9×5 = 45, and 4+5=9). This pattern works indefinitely.

⊚ The number zero was not always accepted in mathematics. Ancient Greeks dismissed it as useless, while Indian mathematicians in the 5th century saw it as revolutionary, eventually introducing it to the world.

⊚ The number 666 is often associated with superstition, but mathematically, it's a "triangular number," meaning it's the sum of all numbers from 1 to 36.

⊚ The Fibonacci sequence appears everywhere in nature, from pinecones and sunflowers to hurricanes and galaxies. Each number is the sum of the two before it, creating a pattern that seems woven into the fabric of the universe.

◎ A perfect number is a number that equals the sum of its proper divisors. The smallest one is 6 (1 + 2 + 3), but they become incredibly rare as numbers grow—so rare that only 60 have been discovered.

◎ The Golden Ratio, approximately 1.618, has fascinated mathematicians, artists, and architects for centuries. Found in living organisms, art, and even the Parthenon, it's often called the "divine proportion."

◎ Ancient Babylonians used a base-60 number system, which is why we divide time into 60 seconds per minute and 60 minutes per hour. Their system was so advanced that they calculated the square root of 2 with surprising accuracy.

◎ The number 7 is often called the "most popular number" due to its frequent appearance in myths, religions, and cultures worldwide. It's the number of continents, wonders of the world, and even dwarfs in *Snow White*.

◎ A prime number is a number greater than 1 that has no divisors other than 1 and itself, but mathematicians still don't know if there's a pattern to their distribution. The largest known prime number has over 24 million digits and was discovered using a supercomputer.

◎ The number π (pi) has been calculated to over 100 trillion digits, but for most calculations, just using 3.14159 is accurate enough. Despite its infinite nature, no repeating pattern has ever been found.

◎ The ancient Greeks thought all numbers could be written as fractions—until they discovered irrational numbers like the square root of 2. This realization was so unsettling that, according to legend, the mathematician who revealed it was drowned at sea.

◎ The Monty Hall Problem, a probability puzzle based on a game show, once baffled even mathematicians. Counterintuitively, switching doors after the host reveals a goat increases your chances of winning from 1/3 to 2/3.

◎ The sum of all natural numbers $(1 + 2 + 3 + 4 \ldots)$ is infinite, but in certain areas of physics, a special technique called analytic continuation assigns it the value -1/12. This strange result appears in string theory and quantum mechanics.

◎ Zeno's paradoxes claim that motion is impossible. One states that to reach a destination, you must first go halfway there, then halfway again, infinitely dividing the distance—meaning you should never actually arrive.

◎ The Tower of Hanoi puzzle, invented in 1883, involves moving stacked discs between three pegs following strict rules. If you started with 64 discs and moved one per second, it would take over 500 billion years to complete.

◎ Mathematicians have been searching for a formula to predict prime numbers for centuries. So far, no one has found a simple way to determine which numbers are prime without checking them one by one.

◎ The Pythagorean theorem is one of the oldest known mathematical rules, but similar concepts were used in Babylon over 1,000 years before Pythagoras was born.

◎ The Riemann Hypothesis is one of the biggest unsolved problems in mathematics. If proven true, it would unlock deep secrets about prime numbers—but so far, no one has cracked it.

◎ Graham's Number is so large that even writing down all its digits would be impossible—the number of digits exceeds the total particles in the observable universe.

◎ The Collatz Conjecture is a simple yet unsolved problem: start with any number, halve it if it's even, or triple it and add 1 if it's odd. Repeat the process, and eventually, you always end up at 1—no one knows why.

◎ The number 2520 is the smallest number that can be evenly divided by all integers from 1 to 10. It's a perfect example of how numbers can fit together in surprising ways.

ENGINEERING WONDERS

◎ The Great Wall of China isn't a single continuous structure but a series of walls and fortifications built over centuries. Some sections were reinforced with sticky rice mortar, an ancient engineering trick that made the walls stronger and more resistant to earthquakes.

◎ The Falkirk Wheel in Scotland is the only rotating boat lift in the world. It lifts boats 79 feet between two canals using Archimedes' principle, requiring minimal energy—just the equivalent of boiling a few kettles of water.

◎ The Millau Viaduct in France is the tallest bridge in the world, with its highest pier standing at 1,125 feet—taller than the Eiffel Tower. The bridge was so precisely engineered that its sections, built separately, aligned perfectly when connected.

◎ The Channel Tunnel (Chunnel) between England and France stretches 31.4 miles under the sea. At its lowest point, it's 250 feet below the seabed, making it one of the longest underwater tunnels in the world.

◎ The Three Gorges Dam in China is the world's largest power station, generating over 100 terawatt-hours of electricity annually. The sheer volume of water it holds has slightly altered the Earth's rotation by redistributing mass.

◎ The International Space Station (ISS) orbits Earth at 17,500 mph, circling the planet every 90 minutes. Its modules, built by different nations, fit together with millimeter precision despite being assembled in space.

◎ The Large Hadron Collider (LHC) is the world's largest machine, a 17-mile-long ring buried underground that smashes particles at nearly the speed of light. The magnets guiding these particles are colder than outer space.

◎ The Panama Canal saves ships an average of 8,000 miles of travel by connecting the Atlantic and Pacific Oceans. Its lock system moves entire ships up and down 85 feet, essentially making them climb over land.

◎ Japan's Shinkansen (bullet trains) were designed to resemble kingfishers to reduce tunnel boom. This bio-inspired tweak allows them to travel at 200+ mph while using less energy and making less noise.

◎ The Hoover Dam contains enough concrete to build a highway from San Francisco to New York. If the dam had been poured all at once instead of in sections, it would have taken over a century to fully cure.

◎ The Sydney Opera House's iconic roof was inspired by the natural shape of an orange. Its architect, Jørn Utzon, solved its complex design by slicing a sphere into segments, making construction possible.

◎ The Golden Gate Bridge is designed to move—its towers can sway up to 27 feet in high winds. Without this flexibility, the structure wouldn't withstand earthquakes or storms.

◎ The CERN data center, which stores information from the Large Hadron Collider, processes data equivalent to 1.7 million DVDs per year. Without powerful algorithms, scientists would drown in raw information.

◎ The Akashi Kaikyō Bridge in Japan is the longest suspension bridge in the world, spanning 12,831 feet. It was originally planned to be shorter, but an earthquake during construction shifted the supporting towers apart by three feet, forcing engineers to adjust the design.

◎ The Palm Jumeirah in Dubai is an artificial island shaped like a palm tree, built using enough sand to fill 2.5 Empire State Buildings. Unlike traditional land reclamation, the sand was precisely sprayed into place using GPS.

◎ The London Underground is the world's oldest subway system, with sections dating back to 1863. In WWII, its tunnels doubled as bomb shelters, housing thousands of Londoners during air raids.

◎ The Itaipu Dam on the Brazil-Paraguay border once held the record for the most hydroelectric power produced in a year—enough to power the entire world for two days. Its construction required moving more earth than was displaced during the excavation of the Panama Canal.

◎ The Bosco Verticale ("Vertical Forest") in Milan is a pair of skyscrapers covered in over 900 trees and 2,000 plants. The greenery improves air quality, lowers temperatures, and dampens noise pollution in the city.

◎ The Mars Rover Curiosity's landing was so complex that NASA engineers called it "seven minutes of terror." It required a heat shield, parachute, retrorockets, and a sky crane working in perfect sequence to gently drop the rover onto the Martian surface.

◎ The Eurotunnel Shuttle, which carries vehicles through the Channel Tunnel, is the longest railway tunnel under the sea. Trains can complete the trip in just 35 minutes, making it faster than flying when factoring in airport delays.

◎ The Beijing Daxing International Airport has the world's largest terminal, covering 7.5 million square feet. Its starfish-like design minimizes walking distances, ensuring travelers never need to walk more than 8 minutes to reach their gate.

◎ The Gotthard Base Tunnel in Switzerland is the longest and deepest railway tunnel, stretching 35.5 miles through the Alps. It took 17 years to complete and allows high-speed trains to pass straight through the mountains rather than winding over them.

◎ The Seikan Tunnel in Japan is the world's longest underwater tunnel for trains, stretching 33.5 miles beneath the sea. It was built to withstand earthquakes and connects Japan's main island to Hokkaido.

◎ The Venice flood barrier system, MOSE, consists of 78 giant metal gates that rise from the seabed when needed. Designed to protect the city from rising sea levels, it took nearly two decades to complete.

◎ The New Safe Confinement structure over Chernobyl's ruined reactor is the largest moveable land-based structure ever built. It was assembled nearby and then slid into place to prevent further radioactive leaks.

◎ The Haliade-X is the world's most powerful wind turbine, standing at 853 feet—taller than the Statue of Liberty. A single rotation of its blades can power a home for two days.

RICH AND FAMOUS

◎ The world's richest dog, Gunther VI, was a hoax. The German shepherd's supposed $500 million inheritance and real estate empire, including a mansion once owned by Madonna, were part of an elaborate publicity stunt—later exposed in the Netflix documentary *Gunther's Millions*.

◎ Pablo Escobar, once one of the richest men in the world, had so much cash that he reportedly spent $2,500 a month just on rubber bands to bundle his money. Rats also ate an estimated $2 billion of his fortune each year.

◎ When Mike Tyson was at the peak of his boxing career, he bought a $2 million solid gold bathtub. He later sold it to an English billionaire's wife as a birthday present.

◎ Oprah Winfrey was once so poor that she had to wear potato sacks as dresses. When she became one of the wealthiest women in the world, she had a designer recreate one of her childhood sack dresses—but this time in high fashion.

◎ Elon Musk once lived on less than $1 a day by eating hot dogs and oranges. Now a billionaire, he still claims to enjoy simple meals— though his definition of "simple" likely includes private chefs.

◎ J.K. Rowling was the first author to become a billionaire solely through book sales. However, she lost her billionaire status—not by losing money, but by donating so much of her wealth to charity.

◎ Warren Buffett, one of the world's richest men, is famously frugal—starting each day with McDonald's breakfast. He chooses his meal based on how the stock market is doing, spending $2.61 on a cheap day and $3.17 when he feels optimistic.

◎ Warren Buffett still lives in the same house he bought in 1958 for $31,500. Despite being one of the world's richest men, he never upgraded to a mansion, calling his modest Omaha home "the third-best investment" he ever made. He once joked that his only regret was not buying two.

◎ In 1923, John D. Rockefeller became the world's first billionaire. Adjusted for inflation, his fortune would be worth over $400 billion today, making him the richest person in modern history.

◎ Archie Karas turned $50 into $40 million in the biggest winning streak in casino history—then lost it all. Over three years in the 1990s, he crushed high-stakes poker and dice games in Las Vegas. But just as quickly, his luck ran out, and he lost everything, ending his legendary run back at zero.

◎ Ronald Wayne, the often-forgotten third co-founder of Apple, sold his 10% stake in the company for just $800 in 1976. Had he kept his shares, they would be worth over $200 billion today. Wayne later said he had no regrets, believing he avoided years of stress—but admitted he wouldn't have minded being "a little richer."

◎ Jack Whittaker won a $314 million Powerball jackpot in 2002, but his fortune quickly turned into a nightmare. He was robbed multiple times, sued, and lost loved ones to tragedy and addiction. Before his death in 2020, he called his lottery win "the worst thing that ever happened" to him.

◎ Bill Gates' home, Xanadu 2.0, took seven years and $63 million to build. The high-tech mansion has a pool with an underwater music system, a trampoline room, and walls that change artwork with the touch of a button.

◎ Kim Kardashian's first job was organizing Paris Hilton's closet. Now a billionaire herself, she hires a team of professionals to do the same for her.

◎ When Jeff Bezos started Amazon in his garage, he kept his desk so cheap that it was just a wooden door on sawhorses. Even after becoming one of the world's richest men, he kept the door desk as a symbol of frugality.

◎ Nicolas Cage once spent $276,000 on a stolen dinosaur skull. When he found out it was illegally smuggled from Mongolia, he returned it—but never got his money back.

◎ The Sultan of Brunei, one of the world's richest royals, owns over 7,000 cars, including more than 600 Rolls-Royces. His collection is worth more than $5 billion, but many of the cars have never even been driven.

◎ Beyoncé and Jay-Z's mansion in Bel-Air has bulletproof windows, four swimming pools, and a helipad. They paid $88 million in cash for it—because billionaires don't bother with mortgages.

◎ Keanu Reeves, despite a net worth of over $300 million, lives modestly and is known for his kindness. He's often seen riding the subway, chatting with fans, and helping strangers, proving that fame and fortune haven't changed him.

◎ Steven Spielberg bought the iconic Rosebud sled from *Citizen Kane* at an auction for $60,500. He later donated it to the Academy Museum of Motion Pictures so it could be preserved as a piece of film history.

◎ Mark Zuckerberg's signature outfit of a gray T-shirt and jeans is no accident—he says wearing the same thing every day eliminates decision fatigue. Ironically, those "simple" shirts are custom-made by an Italian designer and cost hundreds of dollars each.

◎ Zuckerberg stole the idea from Steve Jobs, who wore a black turtleneck, jeans, and sneakers every day. Jobs believed a uniform freed up mental energy, though his attempt to make Apple employees wear matching vests didn't go over so well.

◎ Steve Jobs only took a $1 salary as Apple's CEO, but his wealth came from stock, not paychecks. Most of his fortune didn't even come from Apple—it came from Pixar, which he sold to Disney for $7.4 billion, making him Disney's largest individual shareholder.

◎ The late Saudi King Abdullah once booked out an entire Disneyland theme park for himself and his family. Guests were escorted out early so they could enjoy the rides in complete privacy.

◎ Johnny Depp once spent $3 million to shoot Hunter S. Thompson's ashes out of a cannon. He called it a fitting tribute to the legendary gonzo journalist, who had once joked about wanting to go out with a bang.

◎ Prince Alwaleed bin Talal of Saudi Arabia ordered an Airbus A380— the world's largest passenger plane—just for himself. The custom interior was designed to include a concert hall, a prayer room that rotates to always face Mecca, and a gold-plated throne.

◎ Kylie Jenner became the world's youngest self-made billionaire at age 21, thanks to her cosmetics empire. Critics debated the "self-made" label since she was born into wealth, but her company still made her richer than most of her famous family.

◎ Before winning the lottery, a man in England ate instant noodles every night to save money. After winning $17 million, he continued eating the same noodles—just with fancier toppings like lobster and truffle oil.

◎ Rihanna became a billionaire not from her music but from her cosmetics brand, Fenty Beauty. The company was so successful that within its first year, it outsold Kylie Jenner's beauty line by millions.

◎ Richard Branson once bought a private island for just $180,000 after bluffing about his wealth. He turned it into a luxury resort, where celebrities and billionaires now pay thousands per night to stay.

⊚ Jay Leno never spent a dime of his *Tonight Show* salary, reportedly living only off the money he earned from stand-up comedy. By the time he retired, he had saved over $350 million.

⊚ Michael Jackson once tried to buy Marvel Comics in the 1990s. His dream was to star as Spider-Man in a self-produced movie, but the deal never happened.

⊚ Shaquille O'Neal once spent $70,000 at Walmart in a single shopping spree, the largest purchase in the store's history. The transaction was so large that his bank thought it was fraud and shut down his card.

⊚ Larry Ellison, co-founder of Oracle, owns the entire Hawaiian island of Lanai. He turned it into an eco-friendly paradise with organic farms, luxury resorts, and a commitment to sustainability.

⊚ Madonna once paid $1 million to have a replica of the ceiling from the Sistine Chapel painted inside her home. She later admitted she rarely looked up at it.

⊚ In 2014, Floyd Mayweather bet $10.4 million on a single football game. The risk paid off—he won big, adding to his already massive fortune.

GEOGRAPHICAL WONDERS

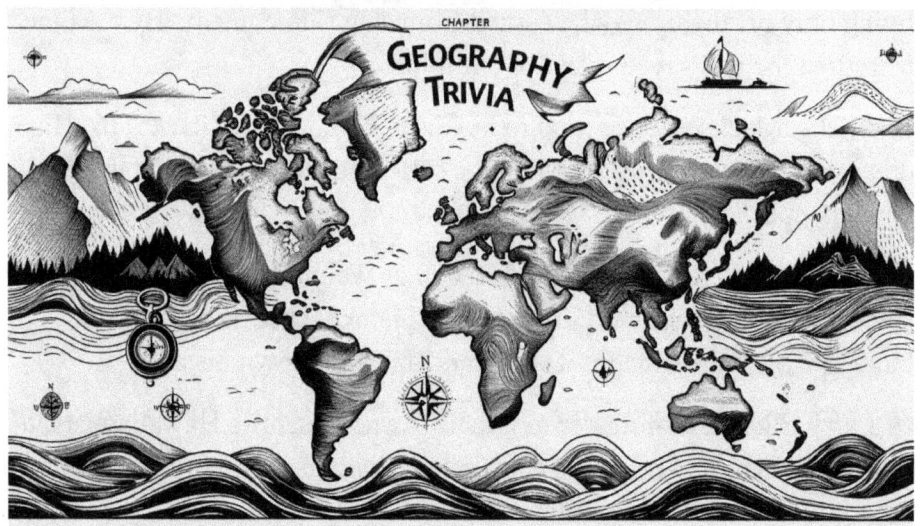

⊚ Mount Everest is still growing. The world's highest peak rises about 4 millimeters per year due to the ongoing collision of the Indian and Eurasian tectonic plates. This means Everest is now taller than when Sir Edmund Hillary and Tenzing Norgay first conquered it in 1953.

⊚ Niagara Falls isn't the tallest waterfall—not even close. Venezuela's Angel Falls holds that title, plunging 3,212 feet—nearly 16 times higher than Niagara. Its water often turns to mist before it reaches the ground.

⊚ There's a waterfall under the ocean. The Denmark Strait Cataract, between Greenland and Iceland, is the world's largest waterfall—but it's entirely underwater. Cold, dense Arctic water plunges 11,500 feet (more than three times the height of Angel Falls) as it flows into the Atlantic.

⊚ The Amazon River didn't always flow east. Millions of years ago, it likely flowed westward—until the gradual rise of the Andes redirected it toward the Atlantic, reshaping the entire South American ecosystem.

⊚ Deep in the Peruvian Amazon, the Shanay-Timpishka river reaches temperatures up to 200°F, hot enough to cook small animals alive. Though far from active volcanoes, its heat comes from underground geothermal springs.

◎ Yellowstone is home to over 60% of the world's geysers, making it one of the most geothermally active places on Earth. The park's supervolcano last erupted 640,000 years ago and remains closely monitored today.

◎ There's a "Door to Hell" in Turkmenistan. A natural gas crater in the Karakum Desert has been burning continuously since 1971. Soviet geologists accidentally set it on fire, thinking it would burn off in days, but more than 50 years later, it's still ablaze.

◎ Antarctica has rivers and waterfalls—that appear to be made of blood. Blood Falls, a crimson-colored stream flowing from Taylor Glacier, gets its eerie color from iron-rich water oxidizing as it hits the air. This bizarre, ancient brine has been sealed under the ice for over a million years.

◎ The Sahara Desert used to be a lush, green paradise. Just 6,000 years ago, the world's largest desert was a fertile savanna with lakes and wildlife. Climate shifts turned it into the barren expanse it is today, but remnants of its green past remain in underground aquifers.

◎ Mount Everest isn't the tallest mountain from base to peak. That title goes to Mauna Kea in Hawaii, which rises over 33,500 feet from its base on the ocean floor—4,000 feet taller than Everest. However, only 13,800 feet of Mauna Kea is above sea level.

◎ A lost continent lies beneath the Indian Ocean. Scientists discovered remnants of "Mauritia," a long-submerged continent buried under lava near Mauritius. It broke off from Madagascar millions of years ago and now exists as scattered crust fragments.

◎ Lake Baikal holds more water than all the Great Lakes combined. The Siberian lake is the world's deepest and oldest freshwater lake, plunging more than a mile deep. It contains about 20% of the planet's unfrozen freshwater supply.

◎ A Mexican river once vanished overnight—and then came back. In 2016, the Río Atoyac in Veracruz mysteriously disappeared into a massive sinkhole, leaving locals baffled. Months later, engineers managed to restore its flow.

◎ There's an island inside a lake, on an island, inside a lake, on an island. Canada's Victoria Island contains a small lake with an island, which itself has a tiny lake with yet another island. It's an extreme example of nature's fractal-like complexity.

◎ Earth's driest place isn't the Sahara—it's in Antarctica. The McMurdo Dry Valleys haven't seen rain for nearly 2 million years. With almost zero humidity, it's one of the closest terrestrial analogs to Mars.

◎ The Grand Canyon has a rival beneath the ocean. The Zhemchug Canyon in the Bering Sea is deeper and wider than the Grand Canyon, but it's hidden under miles of water. If it were on land, it would be one of the largest canyons on Earth.

◎ A river flows through the world's longest cave system. Kentucky's Mammoth Cave is home to an underground river network, including the Green River, which continues to carve new tunnels and chambers beneath the surface.

◎ Beneath the Amazon River lies the "Rio Hamza," a vast underground water system. Though not a fast-moving river, it consists of slow, dense groundwater flowing deep beneath the rainforest.

◎ Mount Chimborazo in Ecuador is technically the highest point on Earth. Because Earth bulges at the equator, Chimborazo's summit is the farthest point from the planet's core—beating Everest by about 7,000 feet.

◎ The Dead Sea is so salty, it forms floating salt crystals. With a salinity of over 30%, it's nearly ten times saltier than ocean water. The dense, mineral-rich waters allow people to float effortlessly while creating bizarre, naturally formed salt sculptures.

◎ The Great Blue Hole in Belize is a massive underwater sinkhole. Over 400 feet deep, this circular abyss was once a dry cave before sea levels rose and flooded it. It's now a diver's paradise, home to rare species and ancient stalactites deep below the surface.

◎ There's a moving island in India. Loktak Lake contains floating masses of vegetation called phumdis, which drift around like natural rafts. Some are large enough to support homes and even a national park.

◎ Earth has a lake with pink water. Australia's Lake Hillier gets its bubblegum hue from salt-loving bacteria that thrive in its ultra-saline environment. Unlike other pink lakes, its color remains vivid even when bottled.

◎ A rock in Saudi Arabia appears to be sliced in half. Al-Naslaa Rock Formation is a massive boulder split with surgical precision, baffling geologists. The nearly perfect split may be due to natural weathering and fault lines.

◎ A mountain in Australia changes color daily. Uluru, also known as Ayers Rock, shifts from deep red to bright orange and even purple depending on the sun's angle. Its dramatic hues come from the oxidation of iron in the rock.

◎ Earth's hottest place isn't Death Valley. Iran's Lut Desert holds the record, with surface temperatures reaching 159°F. It's so inhospitable that even bacteria struggle to survive there.

◎ Iceland has a beach made of black glass. Reynisfjara Beach's jet-black sand comes from pulverized volcanic lava. The contrast between the dark sand and the icy waves makes it one of the most surreal coastlines on the planet.

◎ The Earth has a vast underground ocean. Scientists discovered an enormous reservoir of water locked deep in the mantle, potentially containing more water than all surface oceans combined. But it's trapped in rock, so don't expect any lost Atlantis just yet.

⊚ The Earth isn't a perfect sphere—it's slightly flattened at the poles and bulges at the equator due to its rotation. This means people at the equator are technically farther from the Earth's center than those at the poles.

⊚ The planet's inner core is hotter than the surface of the Sun. At around 10,800°F (6,000°C), it consists mostly of solid iron and nickel, surrounded by a molten outer core.

⊚ More than 70% of the Earth's surface is covered in water, but over 97% of it is salty ocean water. Only about 2.5% of Earth's water is fresh, and most of that is locked in glaciers or underground.

⊚ The Amazon Rainforest produces about 20% of the Earth's oxygen, earning it the nickname "the lungs of the planet." However, the majority of our oxygen actually comes from oceanic phytoplankton.

⊚ The deepest point on Earth is the Mariana Trench in the Pacific Ocean, plunging about 36,000 feet (nearly 7 miles) below sea level. If Mount Everest were placed inside, its peak would still be more than a mile underwater.

⊚ Earth's magnetic field acts like an invisible shield, protecting the planet from harmful solar radiation. Without it, solar winds would strip away the atmosphere, much like what happened to Mars.

⊚ Earth is the only planet in the solar system with plate tectonics. These shifting plates are responsible for earthquakes, volcanoes, and the slow but constant reshaping of continents.

⊚ There are more trees on Earth than stars in the Milky Way. While our galaxy contains about 100-400 billion stars, Earth is home to an estimated 3 trillion trees.

⊚ The Great Barrier Reef, the largest living structure on Earth, is so massive that it can be seen from space. It stretches over 1,400 miles and is home to thousands of marine species.

⊚ The Earth's rotation is gradually slowing down. About 1.4 billion years ago, a day was only 18 hours long, and in a few million years, days will be slightly longer than 24 hours.

⊚ The longest mountain range on Earth is underwater. The Mid-Atlantic Ridge stretches over 40,000 miles along the ocean floor and is more than 10 times longer than the Andes.

⊚ Antarctica is the driest, coldest, and windiest place on Earth. Despite being covered in ice, some regions haven't seen rain or snow in nearly 2 million years.

⊚ A single lightning bolt can reach temperatures five times hotter than the surface of the Sun. Each day, around 8.6 million lightning strikes occur across the planet.

⊚ Earth's atmosphere extends much farther than most people realize. The exosphere, the outermost layer, gradually fades into space and extends over 6,200 miles above the surface.

⊚ The Moon helps stabilize Earth's climate by keeping its axial tilt steady. Without it, Earth's tilt would fluctuate wildly, leading to extreme climate changes over time.

⊚ The highest recorded air temperature on Earth was 134°F (56.7°C) in Death Valley, California, in 1913. The coldest was -128.6°F (-89.2°C) in Antarctica in 1983.

◎ If all of Earth's ice melted, sea levels would rise by about 216 feet, flooding major cities like New York, London, and Shanghai. Luckily, this process would take centuries, but climate change is already accelerating polar ice loss.

◎ There's a massive "gravity hole" in the Indian Ocean where Earth's gravity is weaker than normal. Scientists believe it's caused by ancient magma plumes or the remains of a sunken continent.

◎ More than 90% of volcanic activity on Earth happens underwater. These submarine volcanoes continuously create new ocean floor and sometimes erupt with explosive force.

◎ The oldest known rocks on Earth are over 4 billion years old. Found in Canada, these rocks give scientists clues about what the early Earth was like.

◎ The Pacific Ocean is so vast that it could fit all of the world's continents inside it—with room to spare. It covers more area than all the land on Earth combined.

◎ A small section of the Amazon Rainforest can contain more species of trees than the entire United States. It's home to about 10% of all known species on Earth.

◎ The deepest cave on Earth, Veryovkina Cave in Georgia (the country), plunges more than 7,200 feet underground. It's so deep that a full descent takes multiple days and requires specialized climbing techniques.

◎ The Earth is hit by over 100 tons of space dust every day. Tiny particles from asteroids and comets constantly fall to the surface, unnoticed by most people.

◎ The Grand Canyon is so vast that weather conditions can be completely different at the top and the bottom. The temperature difference between the rim and the canyon floor can exceed 30°F in a single day.

◎ Earth's oceans hold about 20 million tons of gold, but it's so diluted that extracting it would be nearly impossible. Scientists estimate there's roughly one gram of gold per 100 million metric tons of seawater.

◎ If you dug a hole straight through the Earth and jumped in, it would take about 42 minutes to reach the other side—assuming no air resistance and no molten core to incinerate you along the way.

◎ The coldest inhabited place on Earth is Oymyakon, Russia, where temperatures have dropped as low as -96°F (-71°C). Despite the brutal cold, people still live there, and even boiling water freezes mid-air.

PLANT LIFE PECULIARITIES

◎ Some plants can explode. The sandbox tree, also known as the "dynamite tree," produces seed pods that explode with a loud bang, launching seeds at speeds of up to 150 miles per hour. In some cases, the explosion is strong enough to injure nearby animals.

◎ The largest living thing on Earth is a tree. The Pando aspen grove in Utah appears to be a forest of individual trees, but it's actually a single organism connected by an enormous underground root system. Estimated to be over 80,000 years old, it's one of the oldest living things on the planet.

◎ The corpse flower smells as bad as it sounds. The titan arum releases a putrid odor resembling rotting flesh to attract pollinators like carrion beetles. It only blooms once every few years, but when it does, it's one of the most dramatic floral displays in nature.

◎ Bamboo is the fastest-growing plant on Earth. Some species can grow up to 35 inches in a single day. If you listen closely, you might even hear it creak as it stretches toward the sky.

◎ Some trees "bleed" red. The dragon's blood tree, native to Socotra Island, produces a deep red sap that was once believed to have magical properties. Ancient civilizations used it for medicine, dye, and even as a supposed dragon cure-all.

The world's smallest flowering plant is tinier than a grain of rice. Wolffia, or watermeal, floats on the surface of ponds and has flowers so microscopic they can barely be seen with the naked eye. Despite its size, it's packed with protein and is sometimes called "the future of food."

There's a tree that owns itself. In Athens, Georgia, a white oak was legally granted ownership of the land it stands on. The original tree fell in the 1940s, but a new tree, grown from one of its acorns, was planted in its place—and it also owns itself.

The coco de mer palm produces the heaviest seeds in the plant kingdom, sometimes weighing over 90 pounds. These giant seeds were once thought to be treasure from a mythical underwater tree.

A flower in the Arctic can generate its own heat. The Arctic poppy uses its bright yellow petals to focus sunlight toward its center, creating a tiny greenhouse effect. This warmth helps attract pollinators in the frigid tundra.

Some plants can create their own rain. The Amazon rainforest produces so much moisture through transpiration that it helps generate its own weather patterns. If the trees were removed, much of the region could turn into a desert.

The deadliest plant in the world is deceptively pretty. The castor bean plant contains ricin, one of the most toxic substances known to humans. Just a few crushed seeds can be fatal, but in small doses, castor oil from the same plant has been used in medicine for centuries.

Some plants "sweat." On hot days, plants like corn and tomato release excess water through tiny pores, a process called guttation. If you ever see droplets on a plant's leaves in the morning, it's not dew—it's plant sweat.

There's a tree that can walk. The walking palm of the Amazon can slowly move by growing new roots in the direction of sunlight. Over time, it can "walk" several feet to find a better spot.

Some flowers bloom only once every century. The agave, or century plant, spends decades storing energy before producing a massive flower stalk up to 30 feet tall. Once it blooms, it dies, leaving behind seeds for the next generation.

⊚ A plant once went to the Moon. In 1971, astronauts aboard Apollo 14 took seeds from various trees into space. These "Moon Trees" were later planted across the United States and continue to grow today.

⊚ Some plants can produce electricity. The telegraph plant moves its leaves in response to sound vibrations and light, generating tiny electrical currents. Scientists have studied it to create bio-inspired energy sources.

⊚ The world's tallest tree is taller than the Statue of Liberty. A coast redwood named Hyperion in California stands at 381 feet. Its exact location is kept secret to protect it from tourists.

⊚ The sunflower is actually thousands of tiny flowers. Each "petal" is an individual flower, and the center is made up of hundreds of smaller ones, each capable of producing a seed. This makes the sunflower not just one flower, but an entire bouquet.

⊚ There's a tree that can survive being chopped down. The African baobab can regrow from its stump, even if its entire trunk is cut down. Some trees have been known to regrow multiple times over centuries.

⊚ The world's most dangerous tree can cause third-degree burns. The manchineel tree, found in the Caribbean, produces sap so toxic that even standing under it in the rain can blister your skin. Its fruit, known as the "little apple of death," is deadly if eaten.

⊚ Some plants can trap radioactivity. Sunflowers were used after the Chernobyl disaster to absorb radioactive isotopes from contaminated soil. Their roots naturally pull in toxins, making them an unexpected hero in nuclear cleanup efforts.

⊚ The oldest known tree is over 4,800 years old. A bristlecone pine named Methuselah in California predates the Egyptian pyramids. Its exact location is kept secret to prevent vandalism.

◎ Some plants produce caffeine to trick bees. Certain flowers have caffeine in their nectar, which helps bees remember to return. It's nature's way of ensuring pollinators stay loyal.

◎ The lotus can live for thousands of years. Lotus seeds found in ancient Chinese tombs have been successfully germinated after lying dormant for over 1,000 years. They may be some of the longest-living seeds ever discovered.

◎ The vanilla bean is actually a fruit. Despite its name, vanilla comes from an orchid pod, making it more like a tiny banana than a bean. It's also one of the most labor-intensive crops to harvest, which is why real vanilla is so expensive.

◎ A tree in India has the widest canopy in the world. The Great Banyan Tree in Kolkata covers over 18,900 square feet, with aerial roots forming a natural forest-like structure. It's so massive that it has its own postal code.

◎ A plant can mimic an entire ant colony. The *Myrmecodia* plant has hollow chambers inside its stems that ants can live in, providing them shelter in exchange for protection. Some species even produce chemicals that make them smell like ants to avoid being eaten.

NATURE'S ODDITIES

⊚ Wombat poop is cube-shaped, a trait that helps prevent it from rolling away. Scientists believe this helps wombats mark their territory more effectively in the uneven Australian terrain.

⊚ There's a lake in Tanzania called Lake Natron that turns animals into stone. Its highly alkaline waters preserve the bodies of animals that die in it, leaving them eerily mummified and covered in a crusty white shell.

⊚ There's a river in Peru called the Boiling River, where the water reaches temperatures hot enough to cook animals alive. Scientists believe geothermal activity deep underground is responsible, even though it's hundreds of miles from any known volcano.

⊚ A single fungus in Oregon is the largest living organism on Earth. Known as the *Humongous Fungus*, this underground network of mycelium stretches over 3.8 square miles and is estimated to be thousands of years old.

⊚ The Death Valley pupfish has been isolated in a tiny desert pool for thousands of years, surviving in water that regularly reaches over 90°F. Scientists still aren't sure how these fish tolerate such extreme heat and salinity.

◎ The axolotl, a type of salamander, never fully grows up. It retains its juvenile features throughout its life, which is why it looks like a perpetual baby with feathery gills sticking out from its head.

◎ The Dracula ant has the fastest movement of any animal ever recorded. It snaps its mandibles shut at 200 miles per hour, a speed so fast that it defies human perception.

◎ There's a plant called the "Corpse Flower" (*Amorphophallus titanum*) that smells like rotting flesh. It only blooms once every few years, and when it does, it attracts swarms of flies looking for something dead.

◎ A deep-sea creature called the Barreleye fish has a transparent head. Its tubular eyes sit inside its see-through skull, allowing it to look straight up through its own head to spot prey.

◎ In parts of the Sahara, it can get so cold at night that it actually snows. Despite being one of the hottest places on Earth, desert temperatures can plummet below freezing due to a lack of moisture in the air.

◎ The "Zombie Fungus" (*Ophiocordyceps*) takes over the bodies of ants and controls their behavior. Infected ants climb to high places before the fungus bursts out of their heads, spreading its spores to infect more victims.

◎ Deep in the Amazon, there exists a wasp whose sting is described as the most painful insect sting in the world. Known as the *Tarantula Hawk Wasp*, its sting is so intense that victims are advised to "lie down and scream" until the pain subsides.

◎ The mimic octopus can impersonate multiple marine creatures, including sea snakes, lionfish, and flounders. It changes its body shape, movement, and color, fooling predators into thinking it's something far more dangerous than an octopus.

◎ Venus flytraps count how many times an insect touches their hairs before snapping shut. If the prey only touches a hair once, the plant ignores it—but if it touches two or more, the trap clamps down.

◎ Some species of shrimp are naturally bioluminescent and use their glowing spit as a defense mechanism. When threatened, they shoot a glowing blue liquid into the water, temporarily blinding predators and making a quick escape.

◎ There's a lake in Africa called Lake Nyos that can suddenly release a deadly cloud of carbon dioxide, suffocating everything in its path. This rare natural disaster, called a "limnic eruption," has killed thousands of people and animals.

◎ The glacier mouse isn't an animal but a living ball of moss that mysteriously moves across glaciers. Scientists still don't fully understand how these moss clumps stay alive and travel together like tiny herds.

◎ When lightning strikes sand, it can create glass sculptures called fulgurites. These delicate, hollow structures capture the raw power of nature, preserving the lightning's path underground.

◎ The horned lizard has a bizarre defense mechanism—it shoots blood from its eyes. This not only startles predators but also contains chemicals that taste terrible to would-be attackers.

◎ There's a species of jellyfish called the "Pink Meanie" that preys on other jellyfish. Instead of eating plankton like most jellies, it catches and devours entire swarms of smaller jellyfish.

◎ Some trees can "talk" to each other using underground fungal networks. These networks, often called the "Wood Wide Web," allow trees to share nutrients, warn of danger, and even support sick neighbors.

◎ The water bear, or tardigrade, is one of the toughest creatures on Earth. It can survive boiling heat, freezing temperatures, the vacuum of space, and even radiation levels that would kill most life forms.

ACCIDENTAL INVENTIONS

◉ The waffle iron inspired the invention of Nike's first running shoes. Bill Bowerman, a track coach, poured rubber into his wife's waffle maker to create a better-gripping sole, leading to the first Nike "Waffle" sneakers.

◉ The accidental invention of the microwave happened when a scientist noticed a chocolate bar had melted in his pocket while standing near a radar device. A quick test with popcorn kernels confirmed that microwaves could cook food, and the kitchen revolution was born.

◉ The Post-it Note was a failed experiment. A scientist at 3M, Spencer Silver, was trying to create a super-strong adhesive but accidentally made one that barely stuck. Years later, his colleague realized it was perfect for reusable sticky notes.

◉ Penicillin, the first antibiotic, was discovered when Alexander Fleming left a petri dish of bacteria uncovered near an open window. When he returned, he found mold killing the bacteria, leading to one of the most important medical breakthroughs in history.

◉ The pacemaker exists thanks to a wrong-sized resistor. Wilson Greatbatch, working on a heart rhythm recording device, accidentally inserted the wrong part, and it started mimicking a heartbeat, leading to the first implantable pacemaker.

◎ Potato chips were invented in 1853 when a chef, George Crum, got frustrated with a picky customer who kept sending back his fries for being too thick. To annoy him, Crum sliced the potatoes paper-thin and fried them until crispy—only for the customer to love them.

◎ Super Glue was discovered by accident—twice. During World War II, scientists were trying to develop clear plastic gun sights when they stumbled upon a chemical that stuck to everything. It was dismissed until years later when it was recognized as a powerful adhesive.

◎ Coca-Cola started as a medicinal tonic. In 1886, pharmacist John Pemberton was trying to make a headache cure but accidentally mixed coca leaf extract with carbonated water, creating the first batch of Coke.

◎ Safety glass was invented when a scientist dropped a flask and it didn't shatter. French chemist Édouard Bénédictus realized the glass had been coated with a plastic film that held the shards together, leading to modern shatterproof glass.

◎ The first synthetic dye was discovered when an 18-year-old chemist, William Perkin, was trying to create a cure for malaria. Instead, he accidentally made a vibrant purple dye, revolutionizing the fashion industry.

◎ Velcro was inspired by burrs stuck to a dog's fur. Swiss engineer George de Mestral examined the tiny hooks on the burrs under a microscope and used the design to create the now-famous fastener.

◎ Corn Flakes were invented when two brothers, John and Will Kellogg, accidentally left cooked wheat sitting out overnight. When they rolled it the next morning, it crumbled into flakes, leading them to create the first ready-to-eat breakfast cereal.

◎ The popsicle was invented by an 11-year-old. In 1905, Frank Epperson accidentally left a cup of soda with a stirring stick outside in the cold overnight. The next morning, he had a frozen treat—and decades later, he patented it.

◎ X-rays were discovered when Wilhelm Roentgen noticed a mysterious glow coming from a cathode-ray tube. When he placed his hand in front of it, he saw his bones projected onto a screen, leading to the first medical X-ray.

◎ The ice cream cone was created out of necessity at the 1904 World's Fair. A vendor ran out of cups, so a nearby waffle seller rolled his waffles into cones to hold the ice cream, creating an instant hit.

◎ LSD was discovered by accident when chemist Albert Hofmann absorbed a tiny amount through his skin while researching medicinal compounds. The unexpected effects led to the world's first psychedelic trip.

◎ Saccharin, the first artificial sweetener, was found when a scientist forgot to wash his hands. After working with coal tar derivatives, Constantine Fahlberg ate dinner and noticed his bread tasted oddly sweet.

◎ Stainless steel was invented when a British metallurgist, Harry Brearley, was trying to develop a better gun barrel. He discovered that an iron-chromium alloy resisted rust, leading to the creation of stainless steel.

◎ The modern match was created when an English chemist, John Walker, accidentally scraped a chemical-coated stick against his workbench and it ignited. He never patented it, but the idea quickly spread.

◎ Anesthesia was discovered when people at laughing gas parties noticed they weren't feeling pain. Doctors realized nitrous oxide could be used in surgery, changing the world of medicine forever.

◎ The microwave-safe Tupperware lid was discovered when a scientist, Earl Tupper, was experimenting with plastic scraps from a petroleum company. His material was flexible yet durable, leading to the iconic airtight food container.

◎ Smart dust—tiny sensors used for tracking and surveillance—was invented when a scientist's experiment exploded, scattering microscopic particles. Instead of a disaster, it became the foundation of cutting-edge technology.

◎ The artificial heart was partly inspired by car mechanics. Engineer Paul Winchell, fascinated by how pistons worked in car engines, used a similar concept to design the first artificial heart prototype.

◎ The first GPS was created using a scientific prank. Two physicists were tracking Sputnik for fun when they realized they could pinpoint its location based on radio signals—leading to the development of global positioning technology.

◎ The origins of chewing gum date back thousands of years, but the first modern gum was made accidentally. In the 1860s, a scientist trying to create a new rubber substitute ended up with a chewy, stretchable material that became gum.

◎ The rubber glove was created when a doctor's wife developed a skin allergy to surgical chemicals. To protect her hands, he ordered thin rubber gloves from Goodyear, revolutionizing medical safety.

SMALL CHANGES, BIG IMPACT

◎ When NASA engineers switched from imperial to metric measurements in 1999, they forgot to update one crucial calculation for the Mars Climate Orbiter. The result? The $125 million spacecraft burned up in the Martian atmosphere due to a conversion error.

◎ A single vote has changed the course of history more than once. In 1923, a one-vote margin in the German Reichstag played a crucial role in blocking an attempt to ban the Nazi Party, allowing Adolf Hitler to continue his rise to power. A decade later, narrow political maneuvering enabled Hitler to assume dictatorial control, leading to World War II.

◎ The introduction of the potato to Europe in the 16th century led to a population boom. This simple crop provided more calories per acre than wheat, fueling an unprecedented increase in European populations. Without it, some historians argue the Industrial Revolution may have been delayed.

◎ In 1907, a Boston doctor began washing his hands before delivering babies. Mortality rates for newborns at his hospital plummeted from 18% to 2%. The medical community ignored his findings for decades, costing thousands of lives.

⊚ The 1881 assassination of President James Garfield could have been survivable, but doctors kept probing his wound with unwashed hands, causing fatal infections. A small change—washing hands and sterilizing instruments—would have likely saved his life.

⊚ A tiny genetic mutation 10,000 years ago allowed humans to digest lactose as adults. Before that, drinking milk past childhood caused severe digestive issues. Today, over 90% of northern Europeans carry this mutation, while most East Asians remain lactose intolerant.

⊚ The switch from leaded to unleaded gasoline in the 1970s had an unexpected effect: crime rates dropped dramatically. Studies suggest that removing lead from the environment improved cognitive function and reduced aggression, making society less violent overall.

⊚ In 1965, Ralph Nader's book *Unsafe at Any Speed* led to the mandatory use of seat belts in cars. The small change of wearing a seat belt has since saved over 375,000 lives in the U.S. alone.

⊚ A clerical error in 1879 added an extra "s" to the name of a company, turning "Standard Oil Company" into "Standard Oil Companies." This minor mistake allowed John D. Rockefeller to argue in court that he wasn't running a monopoly, delaying antitrust action against him for years.

⊚ A typo in a genetics study once suggested humans share 99.9% of their DNA with bananas. The real number? Closer to 60%. Still impressive, but not quite as eyebrow-raising.

⊚ The Spanish flu of 1918 was not actually Spanish—it got its name because Spain was neutral in World War I and freely reported on the outbreak. Other nations suppressed news to maintain morale, making it seem like Spain was the only country affected. A simple policy shift could have changed history.

⊚ When Britain switched from the Julian to the Gregorian calendar in 1752, they skipped 11 days. Some people believed their lives had been shortened and even rioted in the streets, demanding their "missing days" back.

⊚ The modern tomato wasn't always red. Originally, tomatoes were small, yellow, and bitter, but selective breeding over centuries made them the juicy red staple we know today.

⊚ In 1980, a simple change in hospital policies led to a 50% reduction in newborn deaths. Instead of isolating premature babies, doctors began practicing "kangaroo care," placing infants on their mothers' chests for warmth and bonding.

⊚ A small mistake in Napoleon's invasion plans led to one of the worst military disasters in history. His mapmakers miscalculated the Russian winter, failing to provide enough supplies for his troops. Of the 600,000 soldiers who marched into Russia, fewer than 50,000 survived.

⊚ The 1854 cholera outbreak in London was stopped not by doctors, but by a simple act of removing the handle from a contaminated water pump. Dr. John Snow's investigation showed that contaminated water, not "bad air," caused cholera—revolutionizing public health.

⊚ The modern pencil exists because of a storm. In 1565, a tree was blown over in England, exposing a deposit of pure graphite. Locals began using the material for writing, leading to the invention of the pencil as we know it today.

⊚ The switch from kerosene to electricity for lighting led to a surprising benefit: fewer whale deaths. In the 19th century, whale oil was the primary fuel for lamps, driving mass whale hunting. The invention of the light bulb helped save entire species.

⊚ A tiny change in 19th-century postage rates led to a boom in letter-writing. When the cost of sending a letter dropped to two cents, mail became more affordable, and people wrote more often—strengthening relationships across long distances.

⊚ The simple addition of iodine to salt in the 1920s dramatically reduced cases of goiter (an enlarged thyroid) worldwide. Before that, iodine deficiency caused widespread health problems, but this small dietary tweak nearly eradicated the condition in many regions.

◎ A single lightbulb helped solve a murder in 1912. Investigators at the Villisca axe murder house noticed that the killer had removed the bulb from the front porch, ensuring no one would see him enter. This small detail became a crucial clue in understanding the crime.

◎ The introduction of the cotton gin made cotton production vastly more efficient, but it also had unintended consequences. By making cotton farming more profitable, it strengthened slavery in the American South, prolonging the practice for decades.

◎ The modern keyboard layout (QWERTY) was designed to slow typists down, not speed them up. Early typewriters jammed when people typed too fast, so the layout was intentionally inefficient.

◎ In 1967, Sweden switched from driving on the left to the right side of the road overnight. Despite fears of chaos, the transition was surprisingly smooth, with fewer accidents than usual in the days following the change.

POPULAR MUSIC

◎ Elvis Presley's first major hit, *Heartbreak Hotel* (1956), was inspired by a real-life suicide note that simply read, "I walk a lonely street." The song's haunting sound helped make it one of the most influential rock songs of all time.

◎ The Beatles hold the record for the most number-one hits on the Billboard Hot 100, with 20 songs reaching the top. Their final chart-topper, *The Long and Winding Road* (1970), was released after the band had already broken up.

◎ *Johnny B. Goode* by Chuck Berry (1958) was the first rock-and-roll song sent into space. It was included on the Golden Record aboard the Voyager spacecraft as part of humanity's message to potential extraterrestrial life.

◎ Bob Dylan shocked fans at the 1965 Newport Folk Festival by playing an electric guitar for the first time. Folk purists booed him, but the moment marked a turning point in rock history.

◎ The Rolling Stones' iconic tongue-and-lips logo was inspired by the Hindu goddess Kali. Designed by John Pasche in 1970, it became one of the most recognizable band logos in history.

⊚ Jimi Hendrix's performance of *The Star-Spangled Banner* at Woodstock (1969) was entirely improvised. He used feedback and distortion to mimic the sounds of war, turning the anthem into a powerful anti-war statement.

⊚ Queen's *Bohemian Rhapsody* (1975) took three weeks to record and features over 180 vocal overdubs. Freddie Mercury refused to explain the song's meaning, saying it was simply "about relationships."

⊚ David Bowie's *Space Oddity* (1969) was released just days before the Apollo 11 moon landing. The BBC initially banned it due to its dark ending but later used it during their coverage of the event.

⊚ The Bee Gees didn't originally set out to make disco music. Their falsetto-driven sound, which became their signature, was discovered by accident while recording *Nights on Broadway* (1975).

⊚ Michael Jackson's *Thriller* (1982) remains the best-selling album of all time, with over 70 million copies sold. The groundbreaking 14-minute music video cost $500,000 to make—an enormous sum for a music video at the time.

⊚ Madonna's *Like a Prayer* (1989) music video, featuring religious imagery and burning crosses, was so controversial that Pepsi canceled a $5 million sponsorship deal with her. The song became one of her biggest hits despite the backlash.

⊚ Prince played 27 instruments on his debut album, *For You* (1978). He was so controlling over his music that he often recorded entire albums alone, playing every instrument himself.

⊚ Nirvana's *Nevermind* (1991) was expected to sell about 250,000 copies but went on to sell over 30 million. The success of *Smells Like Teen Spirit* marked the beginning of grunge's mainstream dominance.

⊚ The Red Hot Chili Peppers' *Give It Away* (1991) was inspired by a life lesson from Nina Hagen. She once gave lead singer Anthony Kiedis a jacket, teaching him that generosity brings good energy.

◎ Whitney Houston's *I Will Always Love You* (1992) spent 14 weeks at number one, making it one of the longest-running chart-toppers. The song was originally written and recorded by Dolly Parton.

◎ *Wonderwall* (1995) remains Oasis's most famous song, but lead singer Liam Gallagher has said he doesn't even like it. His brother and bandmate Noel wrote it for his then-wife, but the two later divorced.

◎ *Stan* (2000) by Eminem was so influential that the term "stan" is now used to describe obsessive fandom. The song was inspired by real letters from fans and features a sample of Dido's *Thank You.*

◎ *Lose Yourself* (2002) was the first rap song to win an Academy Award for Best Original Song. Eminem was so convinced he wouldn't win that he didn't even attend the ceremony.

◎ *Crazy in Love* (2003) was written in just two hours. Beyoncé wasn't initially a fan of the song's horn intro, but it became one of the most recognizable hooks in pop music.

◎ The Weeknd's *Blinding Lights* (2019) is the longest-charting song in Billboard Hot 100 history, spending over 90 weeks on the chart. The song's synth-driven sound was inspired by 1980s pop music.

◎ *Rolling in the Deep* (2010) by Adele was written after a painful breakup. The song's raw emotion helped it become one of the best-selling digital singles of all time.

◎ *Seven Nation Army* (2003) by The White Stripes became an unofficial sports anthem worldwide. The riff was so catchy that fans in stadiums began chanting it, turning it into a global phenomenon.

◎ Taylor Swift became the first artist in history to occupy the entire top 10 of the Billboard Hot 100 with songs from *Midnights* (2022). No other artist has achieved this feat in the chart's 60+ year history.

◎ The Eagles' *Hotel California* (1976) was recorded in just one take. The song's mysterious lyrics have led to endless theories, but Don Henley insists it's about "the dark side of the American Dream."

◎ U2's *The Joshua Tree* (1987) was the first album to sell over a million copies on CD alone. The album cover was shot in the Mojave Desert, but the famous tree in the photo has since fallen over due to age.

◎ Metallica's *Enter Sandman* (1991) was originally written as a song about sudden infant death syndrome, but the lyrics were changed to make it less disturbing. It remains one of the band's biggest hits.

◎ *Hey Jude* (1968) was originally written by Paul McCartney to comfort John Lennon's son Julian during his parents' divorce. The song's extended outro makes it one of the longest number-one hits ever.

◎ *We Will Rock You* (1977) was intentionally written with a stomp-clap beat so audiences could participate. The song has since become a stadium anthem, played at countless sporting events worldwide.

◎ *Sweet Child o' Mine* (1987) by Guns N' Roses started as a joke when Slash was warming up on his guitar. The rest of the band turned it into a full song, making it one of their biggest hits.

◎ *Let It Be* (1970) was inspired by a dream Paul McCartney had about his mother, who had died when he was a teenager. The phrase "Let it be" was something she told him in the dream.

◎ *Candle in the Wind 1997*, written in memory of Princess Diana, is the best-selling single of all time. It sold over 33 million copies worldwide, with all proceeds donated to Diana's charities.

◎ *Shallow* (2018) by Lady Gaga and Bradley Cooper won the Oscar for Best Original Song. Cooper took singing lessons for months to prepare, but Gaga insisted they sing live rather than lip-sync.

◎ Billie Eilish recorded *Bad Guy* (2019) in her bedroom with her brother Finneas producing. The song's distinctive bassline was created with a simple keyboard effect.

◎ Fleetwood Mac's *Rumours* (1977) was recorded while the band members were going through personal breakups. The emotional tension fueled hits like *Go Your Own Way* and *Dreams*, making it one of the best-selling albums ever.

MUSIC HISTORY

The Historic 1920 Radios Radioi Broadcast

KDKA

⊚ Thomas Edison's invention of the phonograph in 1877 changed the music industry forever. The first recording he ever made was of him reciting "Mary Had a Little Lamb."

⊚ The first recorded piece of music dates back over 3,400 years. A hymn inscribed on a clay tablet, known as the *Hurrian Hymn No. 6*, was discovered in ancient Ugarit (modern-day Syria) and is the oldest known example of written music.

⊚ Scott Joplin's *Maple Leaf Rag* (1899) was the first sheet music to sell over one million copies. His mastery of ragtime piano laid the groundwork for jazz and influenced generations of musicians.

⊚ The first commercial radio broadcast in 1920 featured music from a phonograph. It was broadcast by KDKA in Pittsburgh, marking the beginning of radio as a mass entertainment medium.

⊚ The first jazz recording, *Livery Stable Blues* (1917) by the Original Dixieland Jass Band, was also the first song to be labeled "jazz." Despite its popularity, many early jazz pioneers—particularly Black musicians—weren't given the same recognition.

⊚ Blues music originated in the Deep South in the late 19th century, blending African musical traditions with spirituals and work songs. The first recorded blues song, *Crazy Blues* by Mamie Smith (1920), opened the doors for Black musicians in the recording industry.

⊚ Louis Armstrong revolutionized jazz in the 1920s with his groundbreaking trumpet playing. His 1928 recording of *West End Blues* introduced improvisation as a key element of jazz, changing the genre forever.

⊚ The first country music recording was made in 1922 by Eck Robertson, a fiddler from Texas. However, it was Jimmie Rodgers, the "Father of Country Music," who made the genre a national sensation with his 1927 hit *Blue Yodel No. 1 (T for Texas)*.

⊚ Bessie Smith, the "Empress of the Blues," was one of the highest-paid Black performers of the 1920s. Her powerful voice and dramatic delivery made songs like *Downhearted Blues* (1923) legendary.

⊚ The first film with synchronized sound, *The Jazz Singer* (1927), featured Al Jolson performing popular songs. While revolutionary for the time, its use of blackface remains a controversial stain on music and film history.

⊚ Duke Ellington's residency at the Cotton Club in the 1920s helped shape swing music. His orchestra introduced a sophisticated, jazz-infused big band sound that dominated the 1930s and 1940s.

⊚ *Strange Fruit* (1939) by Billie Holiday was one of the first protest songs in American music history. The haunting song, which depicts the horrors of lynching, was so controversial that many radio stations refused to play it.

⊚ Robert Johnson, the legendary blues guitarist, recorded only 29 songs before his mysterious death at age 27. His rumored deal with the Devil at the crossroads remains one of the most famous myths in music history.

⊚ The Grand Ole Opry, founded in 1925, is the longest-running live radio show in history. Originally called the *WSM Barn Dance*, it played a crucial role in the rise of country music.

◎ The world's first pop star, Bing Crosby, sold over 500 million records during his career. His 1942 recording of *White Christmas* remains the best-selling single of all time.

◎ *Boogie Woogie* piano, which heavily influenced rock and roll, originated from barrelhouse blues. The first boogie-woogie hit, *Pinetop's Boogie Woogie* (1928), gave the genre its name and set the stage for future rock pioneers.

◎ Glenn Miller's *In the Mood* (1939) became one of the most recognizable songs of the swing era. Miller's smooth, tightly arranged sound defined the World War II generation.

◎ In 1948, Columbia Records introduced the first 33⅓ RPM vinyl LP, replacing fragile shellac records. This allowed for longer albums and revolutionized the way people listened to music.

◎ *La Vie en Rose* (1947) became Edith Piaf's signature song and one of the most beloved recordings in French music history. Despite her tragic life, Piaf's voice captured the essence of romance and resilience.

◎ Western swing, a mix of country, jazz, and blues, was pioneered by Bob Wills and His Texas Playboys in the 1930s. Their hit *San Antonio Rose* became a crossover success, influencing generations of country artists.

◎ The first electronic instrument, the theremin, was invented in 1920 by Russian scientist Leon Theremin. It was played without physical contact and later became a staple of eerie sci-fi soundtracks.

◎ *This Land Is Your Land* (1940) by Woody Guthrie was written as a response to Irving Berlin's *God Bless America*, which Guthrie felt was too idealistic. His version became one of America's most enduring folk songs.

◎ The Ink Spots' smooth vocal harmonies in the 1930s helped lay the groundwork for rhythm and blues. Their hit *If I Didn't Care* (1939) remains one of the best-selling singles of all time.

◎ Billie Holiday was one of the first singers to use a microphone as an expressive instrument. Her subtle phrasing and emotional delivery changed vocal jazz forever.

◎ The *Big Bang of Country Music* happened in 1927 when talent scout Ralph Peer recorded The Carter Family and Jimmie Rodgers in Bristol, Tennessee. These sessions helped define country music as a genre.

◎ In 1942, the U.S. government temporarily banned the recording of new music due to a musician's union strike. This led to the rise of a cappella performances and wartime re-releases of older songs.

◎ The Weavers' *Goodnight, Irene* (1950) helped revive folk music in mainstream America. The song introduced folk to a wider audience, paving the way for artists like Bob Dylan and Joan Baez.

◎ Frank Sinatra's *bobby soxer* fans in the 1940s were the first modern pop music superfans. His concerts caused near riots, setting the stage for Beatlemania two decades later.

◎ The first official Billboard chart appeared in 1940, ranking the top-selling records in the U.S. Before that, sales data was unreliable, with many music charts based on jukebox plays and sheet music sales.

COUNTRY MUSIC

⊚ Hank Williams wrote *Your Cheatin' Heart* (1952) while driving in a car with his wife. He described the lyrics as an autobiographical confession, and the song became one of the most influential in country music history.

⊚ Johnny Cash's *Folsom Prison Blues* (1955) was inspired by a real prison documentary he saw while serving in the Air Force. When he performed it live at Folsom Prison in 1968, the cheering inmates nearly drowned out the song.

⊚ Dolly Parton wrote *Jolene* and *I Will Always Love You* on the same day. *I Will Always Love You* later became one of the best-selling songs of all time after Whitney Houston's 1992 cover.

⊚ Willie Nelson wrote *Crazy* (1961), but he never had a hit with it. Instead, Patsy Cline recorded it, and it became one of the most-played jukebox songs in history.

⊚ *He Stopped Loving Her Today* (1980) by George Jones is often called the greatest country song ever written. Jones hated the song at first and refused to record it, only to see it revive his career.

◎ Loretta Lynn's *Coal Miner's Daughter* (1970) is a true story about her childhood in rural Kentucky. The song became so iconic that it was turned into an Oscar-winning movie starring Sissy Spacek.

◎ Garth Brooks is the best-selling solo artist in U.S. history, surpassing Elvis Presley. His album *Double Live* (1998) is the best-selling live album of all time, with over 21 million copies sold.

◎ Reba McEntire's *Fancy* (1990) was originally recorded by Bobbie Gentry in 1969. The song, about a mother who encourages her daughter into a life of luxury, became Reba's signature anthem.

◎ Merle Haggard was inspired to write *Mama Tried* (1968) after spending time in San Quentin Prison. He was once an inmate while Johnny Cash performed there, and the experience pushed him to change his life.

◎ Kenny Rogers' *The Gambler* (1978) was written by Don Schlitz, who was only 23 at the time. The song was so influential that Rogers later starred in a series of TV movies based on its lyrics.

◎ Tammy Wynette's *Stand By Your Man* (1968) was written in just 15 minutes. Despite controversy over its lyrics, it became one of the most recognized country songs ever recorded.

◎ *Take Me Home, Country Roads* (1971) was inspired by a road in Maryland, not West Virginia. However, John Denver's love for the state made it an unofficial West Virginia anthem.

◎ Charley Pride was one of the first Black country music stars, breaking racial barriers in the 1960s. His song *Kiss an Angel Good Mornin'* (1971) became his biggest hit and crossed over into the pop charts.

◎ The Grand Ole Opry banned Hank Williams in 1952 due to his drinking problems. He was never officially reinstated, but his influence remains one of the strongest in country music history.

◎ Taylor Swift started as a country artist before transitioning into pop. Her early hits like *Tim McGraw* (2006) and *Our Song* (2007) helped bring a younger audience to country music.

◎ Johnny Cash's *Ring of Fire* (1963) was written by June Carter about her forbidden love for Cash. The song's signature mariachi horns were suggested by Cash after a dream about hearing the sound.

◎ Shania Twain's *Come On Over* (1997) is the best-selling country album of all time. With over 40 million copies sold worldwide, it helped bring country music to an international audience.

◎ Kris Kristofferson wrote *Me and Bobby McGee* (1969) while sweeping floors at Columbia Studios. Janis Joplin recorded it shortly before her death, and it became a posthumous number-one hit.

◎ Waylon Jennings was supposed to be on the plane that crashed and killed Buddy Holly in 1959. He gave up his seat to The Big Bopper and later struggled with survivor's guilt.

◎ *Achy Breaky Heart* (1992) by Billy Ray Cyrus sparked a global line-dancing craze. It was also the first country single to be certified platinum since Kenny Rogers' *The Gambler*.

◎ *9 to 5* (1980) by Dolly Parton was written by tapping her fingernails together like a typewriter sound. The song became an anthem for working women and won two Grammy Awards.

◎ Luke Bryan started out as a songwriter, penning hits for artists like Travis Tritt before launching his own career. He is now one of the top-selling country artists of the 21st century.

◎ Johnny Paycheck's *Take This Job and Shove It* (1977) became a working-class anthem. The phrase entered everyday language, often used by frustrated employees quitting their jobs.

◎ Carrie Underwood is the only solo country artist to have every studio album debut at number one on the Billboard Country Chart. She rose to fame after winning *American Idol* in 2005.

◎ Florida Georgia Line's *Cruise* (2012) is the best-selling digital country song of all time. The remix featuring Nelly helped push country music into the pop and hip-hop markets.

◎ Hank Williams Jr.'s *All My Rowdy Friends Are Coming Over Tonight* (1984) became the theme song for *Monday Night Football* for over 20 years. The song became synonymous with football season.

◎ Chris Stapleton's *Tennessee Whiskey* (2015) was originally recorded by David Allan Coe in 1981. Stapleton's bluesy version made it a modern-day classic and a karaoke favorite.

◎ Dolly Parton turned down Elvis Presley's request to record *I Will Always Love You* because his manager demanded half the publishing rights. It was a tough decision, but years later, Whitney Houston's version made it one of the most successful songs in history.

◎ Willie Nelson's braids were once auctioned for $37,000. The legendary singer cut them off in the 1980s and later used them to raise money for charity.

The gunfight at the O.K. Corral, one of the most famous shootouts in history, lasted only about 30 seconds. Despite the legend, it wasn't a classic showdown in the middle of the street—it happened in a narrow alleyway behind a corral in Tombstone, Arizona.

Cowboys didn't actually wear cowboy hats as often as movies suggest. Most preferred bowler hats or derby hats, which stayed on better in the wind and were more practical for everyday use.

The Old West had more lawmen than outlaws. Many famous "outlaws," like Billy the Kid, were actually hired as law enforcement at some point in their lives.

Dodge City, Kansas, known as one of the wildest frontier towns, had stricter gun control laws than modern-day Texas. Like many saloons in the Old West, Dodge City had signs that read "Check your guns at the door." Brawls were common, but shootings inside town bars were actually rare.

The Pony Express only lasted 18 months before the telegraph made it obsolete. Despite its legendary status, it was a financial disaster, losing money every month it operated.

◎ Bank robberies were actually rare in the Old West. There were fewer than a dozen confirmed bank heists in all of the frontier towns between 1850 and 1900.

◎ Jesse James was shot in the back by one of his own gang members while straightening a picture on the wall. His killer, Robert Ford, hoped to collect the bounty but was later killed himself.

◎ The first "Wanted: Dead or Alive" poster was for a man named Ben Kilpatrick, a lesser-known outlaw in Butch Cassidy's Wild Bunch. The wording became a staple of Old West bounty posters, even though few actually offered that option.

◎ Tombstone, Arizona, had more churches than saloons in the 1880s. Despite its reputation as a lawless town, it had a strong religious presence and even published multiple newspapers.

◎ Buffalo Bill Cody's famous Wild West show traveled the world, performing in front of royalty, including Queen Victoria. Ironically, the show's version of the Wild West was often more exaggerated than the real thing.

◎ The term "red light district" originated in the Old West. Railroad workers carried red lanterns with them, and when they visited brothels, they left the lanterns outside, giving rise to the term.

◎ Deadwood, South Dakota, was one of the most dangerous towns in the Old West. It was so lawless that Wild Bill Hickok was shot and killed there while holding a poker hand now known as the "Dead Man's Hand"—aces and eights.

◎ Wyatt Earp, famous for the O.K. Corral shootout, later worked as a Hollywood consultant for early Western films. He became friends with young actors like John Wayne, who later shaped the cowboy image in movies.

◎ The Old West was surprisingly diverse. One in four cowboys was Black, Mexican, or Native American, but Hollywood largely erased their contributions from Western films.

◎ The largest gold nugget ever found in the U.S. was discovered in California in 1869. It weighed 195 pounds and was named the "Monumental Nugget."

◎ The real Billy the Kid wasn't the ruthless killer legend made him out to be. He was involved in several shootouts but is only confirmed to have killed one or two people before being gunned down at age 21.

◎ The phrase "riding shotgun" comes from stagecoach days when an armed guard sat next to the driver, ready to fend off bandits and outlaws.

◎ Calamity Jane, one of the most famous female frontierswomen, was known for dressing like a man and exaggerating her exploits. She later toured with Buffalo Bill's Wild West show, blending truth with legend.

◎ The Dalton Gang tried to rob two banks at once in Coffeyville, Kansas, in 1892. The townspeople fought back, killing most of the gang before they could escape.

◎ The Transcontinental Railroad was completed in 1869, linking the east and west coasts for the first time. It reduced travel time across the country from months to just days.

◎ Women in the Old West had more legal rights than in the eastern U.S. States like Wyoming and Montana allowed women to vote and own property decades before the 19th Amendment.

◎ The phrase "burying the hatchet" comes from a Native American custom where tribes would literally bury weapons in the ground as a sign of peace.

◎ The Old West had more dentists than doctors, and "painless dentistry" was often a lie. Many people opted for whiskey or a bullet to bite on instead of anesthesia.

◎ The outlaw Black Bart wasn't your typical bandit—he never shot anyone and left behind polite, poetic notes after robbing stagecoaches.

◎ Many famous gunfights were settled not with shootouts, but with lawsuits. People who were shot often had their families sue for damages, making courtroom battles just as intense as street fights.

◎ Despite popular belief, most cowboys weren't constantly in gunfights. Their real job involved long, exhausting cattle drives, facing more danger from stampedes and weather than from outlaws.

◎ The Texas Rangers, one of the most famous law enforcement groups in the Old West, started with just a few men on horseback. They were originally formed to protect settlers from Native American raids but later became legendary crime fighters.

◎ The famous phrase "Get out of Dodge" comes from Dodge City, Kansas, a notorious frontier town. Lawmen would often tell troublemakers to leave town before they were arrested—or worse.

HISTORICAL TIDBITS

⊚ The CIA once tried to spy on the Soviets with cats. In the 1960s, the CIA launched "Acoustic Kitty," implanting a microphone inside a cat to eavesdrop on conversations. The mission ended quickly when the cat was hit by a taxi on its first assignment.

⊚ Napoleon wasn't actually short. At 5'6" or 5'7", he was average height for his time. The myth of his short stature likely came from British propaganda and a confusion between French and English measurement systems.

⊚ The Eiffel Tower was supposed to be temporary. Built for the 1889 World's Fair, it was meant to be dismantled after 20 years. It only survived because it proved useful as a radio transmission tower.

⊚ A war once lasted only 38 minutes. The Anglo-Zanzibar War of 1896 holds the record for the shortest war in history. It ended when British forces bombarded the sultan's palace, forcing an immediate surrender.

⊚ A cow once caused the Great Chicago Fire—maybe. The infamous blaze of 1871 was long blamed on Mrs. O'Leary's cow kicking over a lantern, but historians now doubt this story. The real cause may never be known, but the fire destroyed over three square miles of the city.

⊚ The Leaning Tower of Pisa started tilting before it was finished. Construction began in 1173, but by the time workers reached the third floor, the foundation had already begun to sink. Engineers spent centuries trying (and failing) to correct its lean.

⊚ The oldest known "yo mama" joke is over 3,500 years old. Written in Babylonian cuneiform, an ancient tablet contains an early example of a joke about someone's mother. Unfortunately, part of the inscription is missing, so the full punchline remains unknown.

⊚ The shortest U.S. presidency lasted just 32 days. William Henry Harrison died of pneumonia in 1841 after delivering a two-hour inaugural speech in freezing weather—without a coat or hat. His successor, John Tyler, was the first vice president to assume the presidency due to a death in office.

⊚ The Titanic's lookouts didn't have binoculars. The ship's key to the storage locker containing the binoculars was accidentally left behind in England. Many believe that if the lookouts had them, they might have spotted the iceberg sooner.

⊚ Ancient Romans used urine to wash their clothes. They collected it in pots on street corners, as the ammonia in urine acted as a natural detergent. Roman laundries even paid a tax on the urine they used.

⊚ In the 18th century, pineapples were a status symbol. Because they were so rare and expensive, people in Europe would rent pineapples just to show them off at parties. Some were never even eaten—just admired until they rotted.

⊚ The Library of Alexandria may not have been destroyed in one fire. While Julius Caesar's siege did burn part of it, historians believe the library's destruction happened gradually over centuries due to neglect, wars, and other fires.

⊚ George Washington's teeth weren't made of wood. His dentures were crafted from a mix of human teeth, cow teeth, and ivory, held together with metal springs. Some of the teeth may have come from enslaved people.

◎ Viking helmets didn't have horns. The classic horned helmet image comes from 19th-century opera costumes, not historical artifacts. Real Viking helmets were simpler, designed for battle rather than theatrics.

◎ The Great Wall of China isn't visible from space. Despite the common myth, astronauts say the wall is difficult to see with the naked eye because it blends in with the natural landscape. However, you can see major cities and road networks from space.

◎ Cleopatra lived closer in time to the iPhone than to the pyramids. The Great Pyramid of Giza was built around 2560 BCE, while Cleopatra ruled Egypt in the first century BCE. More than 2,400 years separated her from the pyramids, but only about 2,000 years separate her from today.

◎ The first recorded use of a flushing toilet was in 1596. It was invented by Sir John Harington, a godson of Queen Elizabeth I. However, the idea didn't catch on until centuries later when indoor plumbing became widespread.

◎ The U.S. once planned to drop a nuclear bomb on the Moon. During the Cold War, the Air Force considered detonating a bomb on the Moon to show military strength. The project, called "A119," was eventually scrapped.

◎ A medieval animal trial once sentenced a pig to death. In 1386, a pig in France was convicted of killing a child and was publicly executed. Such trials were surprisingly common, with various animals being "prosecuted" for crimes.

◎ An emperor once banned coffee. In the 16th century, Ottoman ruler Murad IV made drinking coffee a crime punishable by death. He believed coffeehouses encouraged rebellion—though that didn't stop people from drinking it in secret.

◎ Ancient Egyptians invented breath mints. They mixed cinnamon, myrrh, frankincense, and honey into small pellets to freshen their breath. Pharaohs and nobles carried them in little jars.

◎ The first speeding ticket was issued in 1896. A British man was fined for driving at 8 mph—four times the legal speed limit of 2 mph in towns. His reckless speed terrified pedestrians.

◎ Julius Caesar was once kidnapped by pirates—and he got revenge. When they demanded a ransom, he laughed and told them to ask for more because he was worth it. After he was freed, he returned with an army and had them all executed.

◎ The oldest known musical instrument is over 40,000 years old. A flute made from bird bone was discovered in a cave in Germany. It suggests that early humans enjoyed music long before recorded history.

◎ Winston Churchill once escaped from a prison camp. During the Second Boer War, he was captured in South Africa but managed to slip out of his cell and hop onto a moving train. He later became one of Britain's most famous prime ministers.

◎ The Statue of Liberty almost wasn't in New York. Originally, it was meant for Egypt as a lighthouse for the Suez Canal. When Egypt rejected the idea, the French repurposed the design and gifted it to the U.S. instead.

ANCIENT CIVILIZATIONS

⊚ The Great Pyramid of Giza was the tallest man-made structure in the world for over 3,800 years. It wasn't surpassed until the completion of the Lincoln Cathedral in England in 1311.

⊚ The ancient Sumerians invented the first known writing system, cuneiform, around 3100 BCE. It began as pictographs but evolved into wedge-shaped symbols pressed into clay tablets.

⊚ Roman concrete was so durable that some of their buildings and aqueducts still stand today. Scientists have found that volcanic ash in the mix made it self-healing when exposed to water.

⊚ The Indus Valley Civilization had an advanced sewage and drainage system over 4,000 years ago. Some of their cities had flush toilets and covered drains that rivaled sanitation in 18th-century Europe.

⊚ The ancient Maya had a concept of zero in mathematics centuries before it appeared in Europe. They used a shell symbol to represent it in their complex calendar and counting system.

⊚ The Hanging Gardens of Babylon, one of the Seven Wonders of the Ancient World, may have never existed. No definitive archaeological evidence has ever been found, leading some historians to believe it was a legend.

⊚ Ancient Chinese inventors created the first known seismometer in 132 CE. The device, a bronze urn with dragon heads, could detect earthquakes hundreds of miles away by dropping a ball from a dragon's mouth.

⊚ The Nazca Lines in Peru, massive geoglyphs carved into the desert, were created over 1,500 years ago. Some believe they were astronomical markers, while others think they had religious significance.

⊚ Ancient Egyptian doctors specialized in different fields, much like modern physicians. They had surgeons, dentists, and even ophthalmologists to treat eye conditions.

⊚ The Romans built an extensive road network of over 250,000 miles, many of which are still used today. Their roads were so well-designed that some modern highways follow the same routes.

⊚ The Olmecs, one of Mesoamerica's earliest civilizations, carved massive stone heads weighing up to 40 tons. No one knows exactly how they moved these colossal sculptures without the wheel or metal tools.

⊚ The ancient Persians had an early postal system called the *Angarium*. Couriers rode on horseback, switching at relay stations to deliver messages across the vast empire at remarkable speeds.

⊚ Spartan warriors were trained for battle from the age of seven. They lived in military barracks, enduring harsh discipline, survival training, and combat drills until they became full soldiers at 20.

⊚ The Inca Empire had no written language, but they used a system of knotted cords called *quipu* to record information. The knots represented numbers and may have been used for census data, trade, and history.

⊚ The Phoenicians were expert sailors and are credited with creating one of the first true alphabets. Their writing system influenced Greek and Latin scripts, shaping modern alphabets.

⊚ The Aztecs used cacao beans as currency. They valued chocolate so highly that taxes could be paid in cacao, and counterfeiters would attempt to make fake beans.

⊚ The earliest known peace treaty was signed between the Egyptians and the Hittites in 1259 BCE. The treaty ended years of conflict between the two great powers and is one of the first recorded diplomatic agreements.

⊚ The ancient city of Carthage was so powerful in trade that the Romans destroyed it completely in 146 BCE. Afterward, they spread salt over its land to ensure nothing would grow there again—though this is likely a myth.

⊚ Nero allegedly played the lyre, not the fiddle, while Rome burned in 64 CE. The fiddle didn't even exist yet, but stories of his indifference to the disaster cemented his infamous legacy.

⊚ The Minoans, an advanced civilization on Crete, had multi-story buildings with indoor plumbing over 3,500 years ago. Their palaces featured flushing toilets and underground drainage systems.

⊚ The Celts were known for their intricate gold and bronze jewelry. They had highly skilled metalworkers who created elaborate torcs, bracelets, and weapon decorations.

⊚ The Colosseum in Rome had a retractable awning system called the *velarium*. Sailors operated it to provide shade for spectators during gladiator games.

⊚ The Huns, a nomadic people who terrorized the Roman Empire, were expert horsemen who could ride for days without stopping. Some historians believe they slept on horseback to maintain their speed in battle.

⊚ The first known use of concrete dates back to ancient Mesopotamia, over 5,000 years ago. The Romans later perfected it, using volcanic ash to make it last for millennia.

⊚ The Terracotta Army, built for China's first emperor, Qin Shi Huang, consists of over 8,000 life-sized soldiers. Each warrior has a unique facial expression, making them one of history's greatest artistic achievements.

U.S. PRESIDENTS

⊚ James Madison was the shortest U.S. president, standing just 5 feet 4 inches tall and weighing barely 100 pounds. Despite his small stature, he played a massive role in shaping the U.S. Constitution.

⊚ Andrew Jackson once had a parrot that had to be removed from his funeral because it wouldn't stop cursing. The bird had apparently picked up Jackson's colorful vocabulary over the years.

⊚ Abraham Lincoln was a licensed bartender and co-owned a saloon called "Berry and Lincoln" before entering politics. Unfortunately, the business failed because Lincoln preferred telling stories to customers rather than actually running the bar.

⊚ Ulysses S. Grant was once arrested for speeding—on a horse. The Washington, D.C. police officer who stopped him was nervous about arresting the sitting president, but Grant willingly paid the $20 fine.

⊚ Grover Cleveland personally served as the executioner for two criminals while he was sheriff of Erie County, New York. This earned him the grim nickname "The Buffalo Hangman" before he went on to become president.

⊚ Theodore Roosevelt was shot in the chest while giving a speech but insisted on finishing his 90-minute address before seeking medical help.

The bullet was slowed by 50 pages of speech notes and a metal glasses case in his pocket, likely saving his life.

◎ William Howard Taft once got stuck in the White House bathtub because he was too large to get out on his own. After that incident, an oversized tub was installed to accommodate his 350-pound frame.

◎ Woodrow Wilson was the first sitting president to personally meet the Pope. Before that, American presidents had avoided official meetings with the Vatican due to concerns about religious influence in politics.

◎ Calvin Coolidge had a pet raccoon named Rebecca, originally intended to be eaten for Thanksgiving dinner. Instead of serving her up, he adopted her as a pet and even walked her on a leash around the White House.

◎ Herbert Hoover and his wife, Lou, spoke Mandarin Chinese fluently and often used it to have private conversations in the White House. This skill was particularly useful when they wanted to avoid eavesdroppers.

◎ Franklin D. Roosevelt was the first and only president to serve more than two terms. His four-term presidency led to the creation of the 22nd Amendment, which now limits presidents to two terms.

◎ Harry Truman didn't have a middle name—just the letter "S." It was a compromise between his grandfathers' names, Anderson Shipp Truman and Solomon Young, but it doesn't actually stand for anything.

◎ Dwight D. Eisenhower was a skilled painter and took up art as a stress-relief hobby while in office. His paintings were so well-regarded that he even held an exhibition at the Smithsonian.

◎ John F. Kennedy's famous phrase, "Ich bin ein Berliner," was meant to express solidarity with Berliners during the Cold War. Some claim it translated to "I am a jelly donut," but native Germans understood his intended meaning.

◎ Lyndon B. Johnson used to conduct meetings while sitting on the toilet with the door open. He believed it saved time and kept conversations moving efficiently, though many staffers found it deeply uncomfortable.

⑥ Richard Nixon was a talented musician who could play the piano, violin, clarinet, and accordion. He even performed on national television, playing "Happy Birthday" on the piano for Duke Ellington.

⑥ Gerald Ford is the only person to become U.S. president without ever being elected as president or vice president. He was appointed vice president after Spiro Agnew resigned, then became president when Nixon stepped down.

⑥ Jimmy Carter once filed a report claiming he saw a UFO in 1969. Though he later attributed it to a military aircraft, he remained open to the possibility of extraterrestrial life.

⑥ Ronald Reagan, a former actor, starred in over 50 films before becoming president. His Hollywood career even earned him a Screen Actors Guild presidency before he transitioned into politics.

⑥ George H.W. Bush was the youngest pilot in the U.S. Navy during World War II, earning his wings at just 18 years old. He flew 58 combat missions and was even shot down by the Japanese, surviving hours in the ocean before rescue.

⑥ Bill Clinton won two Grammy Awards—not for singing, but for spoken-word recordings of children's books and historical speeches. One of his wins was for his reading of *Prokofiev: Peter and the Wolf*.

⑥ George W. Bush was once the head cheerleader at his high school in Texas. He later joked that his experience leading pep rallies helped prepare him for leading a nation.

⑥ Barack Obama won a Grammy Award for the audiobook version of his memoir, *Dreams from My Father*. His deep, steady voice later became a trademark of his speeches.

⑥ Donald Trump is the only U.S. president to have a star on the Hollywood Walk of Fame. It was awarded in 2007 for his role as the host of *The Apprentice*.

◎ Joe Biden was the first U.S. president to have a Peloton exercise bike in the White House. Security concerns had to be addressed before he could use it, as the bike's built-in camera and microphone posed a risk.

◎ The White House didn't have running water until the 1830s, during Andrew Jackson's presidency. Before that, all water had to be carried in buckets by staff members.

◎ Martin Van Buren was the first president born as a U.S. citizen. Every president before him was technically born a British subject before the U.S. gained independence.

◎ Chester A. Arthur had over 80 pairs of pants and was known for changing outfits multiple times a day. His extravagant taste in fashion earned him the nickname "Elegant Arthur."

◎ Donald Trump was the first former U.S. president with a criminal record. In May 2024, he was found guilty of 34 felonies during the 2016 presidential campaign. Despite this, he continued his political career and was re-elected in the 2024 election.

HISTORICAL COINCIDENCES

◎ Mark Twain predicted the timing of his own death. He was born in 1835, the same year Halley's Comet passed by Earth. He famously said he'd "go out with it too," and sure enough, he died in 1910, the very day after the comet made its next appearance.

◎ Napoleon and Hitler shared eerie parallels. Both rose to power in their respective countries 129 years apart—Napoleon in 1804 and Hitler in 1933. Both launched invasions of Russia, suffering devastating winter defeats, also 129 years apart (1812 and 1941).

◎ In 1898, author Morgan Robertson wrote a novel called *Futility, or the Wreck of the Titan*, about an "unsinkable" ocean liner named *Titan* that hits an iceberg and sinks. Fourteen years later, the *Titanic* met the exact same fate under eerily similar circumstances.

◎ John Adams and Thomas Jefferson died on the same day. The second and third U.S. presidents both passed away on July 4, 1826—exactly 50 years after the Declaration of Independence was signed. Adams' last words were reportedly, "Thomas Jefferson survives," but Jefferson had died just hours earlier.

◎ The Lincoln-Kennedy coincidences go beyond the obvious. Both were shot in the head on a Friday. Lincoln was shot in Ford's Theatre, while Kennedy was shot in a Ford (a Lincoln Continental).

◎ Edgar Allan Poe may have predicted a real-life tragedy. In his 1838 novel *The Narrative of Arthur Gordon Pym of Nantucket*, shipwreck survivors resort to cannibalism and kill a cabin boy named Richard Parker. In 1884, the *Mignonette* sank, and its desperate survivors also ate their cabin boy—who was named Richard Parker.

◎ The assassination of Archduke Franz Ferdinand had a bizarre twist. After a failed assassination attempt earlier in the day, his driver took a wrong turn and stopped in front of a café—where the assassin, Gavrilo Princip, just happened to be standing. Seizing the opportunity, Princip fired the shots that started World War I.

◎ The sinking of the Lusitania and a newspaper warning. A full-page ad in *The New York Times* warned passengers not to board the *Lusitania*, as it was sailing into a war zone. It was placed by the German embassy. One week later, the ship was sunk by a German U-boat.

◎ The Curse of Tamerlane's Tomb may have started World War II's turning point. Soviet archaeologists opened the tomb of Tamerlane (a brutal conqueror) in 1941, despite warnings that disturbing it would bring destruction. Three days later, Hitler launched Operation Barbarossa, the largest invasion in history.

◎ An American Civil War prophecy eerily came true. Shortly before his death, Confederate General Albert Sidney Johnston reportedly said, "I would give my life for a Southern victory." He was shot in the leg at the Battle of Shiloh, bled out due to an unnoticed wound, and became the highest-ranking officer to die in the war.

◎ A strange connection between Rasputin and the Romanovs. Grigori Rasputin, the mystic advisor to Russia's last imperial family, wrote a letter predicting that if he were murdered by nobles, the Romanovs would be wiped out within two years. He was assassinated in 1916, and two years later, the entire Romanov family was executed.

◎ Wilmer McLean's Civil War story is surreal. The first major battle of the Civil War (Bull Run) began on McLean's farm in Virginia. Seeking peace, he moved 120 miles south—only for the war to literally end in his living room at Appomattox, where Lee surrendered to Grant.

⊚ The Great Chicago Fire and its strange timing. On the same day as the Great Chicago Fire (October 8, 1871), major fires broke out in Wisconsin and Michigan, with the Peshtigo Fire becoming the deadliest wildfire in U.S. history. Some theories suggest a meteor shower sparked them all.

⊚ The first person to be struck by a meteor survived. In 1954, Ann Hodges was hit by a meteorite that crashed through her roof while she was napping. She survived, becoming the only confirmed person in history to be directly struck by space debris.

⊚ In 1864, Union General John Sedgwick scoffed at enemy snipers, declaring, "They couldn't hit an elephant at this distance." Moments later, he was fatally shot in the head by a Confederate sharpshooter.

⊚ The first and last soldiers killed in World War I are buried just feet apart in the same Belgian cemetery. Their graves face each other, despite being killed four years apart.

⊚ Abraham Lincoln's son, Robert Todd Lincoln, was saved from a train accident by Edwin Booth, the brother of John Wilkes Booth, who later assassinated Lincoln. The strange twist of fate was never lost on Robert.

⊚ The Hoover Dam's first and last deaths were exactly 13 years apart—on December 20. Even stranger, the first person to die was J.G. Tierney, and the last was his son, Patrick Tierney.

⊚ The night before John F. Kennedy's assassination, he reportedly had a premonition and told a friend, "If someone wants to kill me, they will do it." The next day, he was shot in Dallas.

⊚ In 1937, aviator Amelia Earhart disappeared over the Pacific, and decades later, skeletal remains were found on an island near her last known location. DNA testing remains inconclusive, keeping her fate a mystery.

⊚ The car Franz Ferdinand was assassinated in had the license plate "A III 118," which some interpret as eerily resembling "Armistice 11-11-18"—the date World War I ended.

⊚ In 1939, a woman named Violet Jessop survived the sinking of the *Titanic* and later survived its sister ship, the *Britannic*, when it was sunk during World War I. She also worked on the *Olympic*, the third sister ship, which suffered a major collision but didn't sink.

⊚ Alexander Graham Bell and Thomas Edison were both obsessed with communicating with the dead. Bell tried to invent a "spirit phone," while Edison worked on a device called the "ghost box." Neither invention succeeded.

⊚ In 1920, a professional baseball game between the Cleveland Indians and the Boston Red Sox was interrupted by a total solar eclipse, plunging the field into darkness. The game resumed once the sun reappeared, making it one of the strangest game delays in history.

⊚ The Roman Empire and the Aztec Empire both peaked with eerily similar government structures, military tactics, and religious practices—despite never having any contact. Some historians call them "parallel civilizations."

STRANGE CONSPIRACY THEORIES

⊚ The Denver Airport is hiding something. Conspiracy theorists believe the airport was built as a headquarters for the New World Order, pointing to its strange murals, massive underground tunnels, and a time capsule set to open in 2094. Even the giant blue Mustang statue outside, known as "Blucifer," adds to the eerie atmosphere—especially since it killed its sculptor.

⊚ Finland doesn't exist. A bizarre theory claims that Finland is just open ocean, and its "existence" is a hoax created by Japan and Russia to allow overfishing in the Baltic Sea. Supposedly, Finnish people actually live in Sweden and just *think* they're in Finland.

⊚ The Titanic never actually sank. Some theorists believe the ship that went down in 1912 was actually the *Olympic*, a nearly identical White Star Line vessel switched in an insurance scam. The theory suggests the company sank the damaged *Olympic* intentionally to claim insurance money.

⊚ The Great Fire of London was an inside job. Some believe the fire of 1666 was deliberately set to destroy poor neighborhoods and allow for a grander reconstruction of the city. Others point to suspiciously well-prepared rebuilding plans as evidence.

◉ The Mandela Effect is proof of parallel universes. The theory suggests that shared false memories—like the spelling of *Berenstain Bears* or whether Monopoly's mascot had a monocle—are evidence of shifts between alternate realities. Some blame this on quantum physics experiments at CERN.

◉ The Large Hadron Collider is a time machine. Theorists claim CERN's massive particle accelerator is actually an attempt to open portals to other dimensions or alter history.

◉ The Beatles were spies. A theory suggests that the Fab Four were secretly working for the British government to spread pro-Western ideals and fight communism. John Lennon's later anti-establishment stance supposedly got him targeted when he outlived his usefulness.

◉ The state of Wyoming is fake. Some conspiracy theorists argue that no one has ever actually met someone from Wyoming, seen it in person, or traveled there intentionally. The joke theory claims it's a government-controlled landmass with a mysterious hidden purpose.

◉ The moon isn't real. A fringe theory suggests that the moon is either a hologram, a disguised spaceship, or a hollow observation post built by extraterrestrials. Some claim this is why NASA never returned to the moon after Apollo 17.

◉ Shakespeare never existed. Some believe that William Shakespeare was actually a collective pen name used by multiple authors—or even a front for Francis Bacon, Christopher Marlowe, or Queen Elizabeth I herself. They argue that no single person could have written such a diverse body of work.

◉ This theory ended up being true. The U.S. government once tried to weaponize the weather. Declassified documents reveal that during the Vietnam War, the U.S. attempted to extend the monsoon season using cloud-seeding technology. The operation, known as *Project Popeye*, aimed to flood enemy supply routes.

◉ Paul McCartney died in 1966. According to this long-running theory, the real Paul was replaced with a lookalike after a fatal car accident.

Clues supposedly appear in Beatles songs, album covers, and even backward-masked recordings.

◎ The 10th planet is hiding behind the sun. Some conspiracy theorists believe in a hidden planet called *Nibiru* that remains unseen because it's always on the opposite side of the sun. Supposedly, when it finally emerges, it will bring catastrophic changes to Earth.

◎ Pigeons are government drones. A satirical theory suggests that all pigeons were secretly replaced by robotic spies. Supporters of the "Birds Aren't Real" movement jokingly claim that birds recharge by sitting on power lines.

◎ A secret planet exists inside Earth. Some believers in the Hollow Earth theory think an entire civilization lives beneath our feet. According to this idea, entrances to the underground world exist at the North and South Poles, which is why Antarctica is so heavily restricted.

◎ The real reason the Library of Alexandria burned was to hide knowledge. Some believe the ancient library held secret information about advanced technology or lost civilizations. According to this theory, powerful groups intentionally destroyed it to suppress humanity's true history.

◎ The Statue of Liberty was originally a disguised lighthouse weapon. A fringe theory claims the statue was designed to emit concentrated beams of light capable of igniting ships from a distance. The supposed death ray never worked, and the statue became a symbol of freedom instead.

◎ The Cold War was staged. Some believe that the U.S. and the Soviet Union were never really enemies, and the entire Cold War was an elaborate scheme to justify military spending. According to this theory, both nations were secretly working together the whole time.

◎ The government controls earthquakes. Some conspiracy theorists believe HAARP (a now-defunct atmospheric research program in Alaska) was secretly designed to trigger natural disasters. Some even claim certain earthquakes and tsunamis were deliberately engineered.

◎ Dinosaurs helped build the pyramids. A bizarre theory suggests that ancient Egyptians domesticated dinosaurs and used them as construction animals. Theorists argue that certain carvings resemble long-necked creatures similar to sauropods.

◉ The 1908 Tunguska explosion was caused by an alien spaceship. The massive blast in Siberia, which flattened 800 square miles of forest, remains a mystery. Some believe it was the crash of an extraterrestrial craft rather than a meteor.

◉ Time travelers caused the downfall of the Roman Empire. Some theorists claim that advanced visitors from the future interfered with Roman politics, causing its eventual collapse. According to this idea, their goal was to prevent Rome from becoming a dominant spacefaring civilization.

◉ NASA astronauts saw something on the moon. Buzz Aldrin and other Apollo astronauts have hinted at unexplained sightings during their missions. Some believe they encountered alien structures or spacecraft but were ordered to keep quiet.

◉ The Mayan calendar didn't predict the end of the world—just a reset. The 2012 phenomenon wasn't about doomsday, but about the end of a cycle in the Mayan Long Count calendar. Some theorists believe that we actually shifted into a new timeline that year without realizing it.

◉ The Bermuda Triangle is a portal to another dimension. Some believe that ships and planes disappear in the area due to a natural time warp, causing them to either vanish or reappear in different places. Others suggest it's an entrance to an underwater alien base.

◉ The moon landing photos were edited—but not faked. Some theorists claim NASA genuinely landed on the moon but had to alter or stage certain photos due to classified technology appearing in the background. According to this theory, some images were touched up to hide what astronauts really saw.

◉ The real Mona Lisa is hidden away. Some conspiracy theorists claim that the painting in the Louvre is actually a copy, while the real masterpiece is locked in a private vault. Some believe this was done to protect the original from theft or damage.

BIGGEST HOAXES

⊚ In 1917, two British girls, Elsie Wright and Frances Griffiths, claimed to have photographed real fairies in their garden. The "Cottingley Fairies" photos fooled even Sir Arthur Conan Doyle, who wrote about them in a magazine. Decades later, the women admitted the fairies were just paper cutouts held up with hatpins.

⊚ The Great Moon Hoax of 1835 tricked thousands into believing astronomers had discovered life on the Moon. A New York newspaper published fake reports describing bat-like humanoids, lush vegetation, and bizarre animals. The hoax was eventually exposed, but not before the paper saw a massive increase in sales.

⊚ In 2002, an artist created a fake "Feejee Mermaid" by sewing a monkey's head and torso onto a fish's tail. This was a recreation of P.T. Barnum's infamous 19th-century hoax, which tricked audiences into believing they were looking at a real mermaid. The grotesque creation was actually just a clever taxidermy stunt.

⊚ The Cardiff Giant, a 10-foot-tall "petrified man," was unearthed in 1869 in New York and hailed as proof of ancient giants. In reality, it was a block of gypsum carved and buried as a prank. Despite being debunked, P.T. Barnum created a replica, claiming the real hoax was the claim that his copy was fake!

◎ In 1938, a radio broadcast of H.G. Wells' *The War of the Worlds* caused panic as listeners thought Martians were invading Earth. Though later exaggerated, some people did flee their homes or jam emergency lines. The mass hysteria was largely fueled by newspapers looking to discredit radio as a new medium.

◎ Piltdown Man was one of the biggest scientific hoaxes of all time, fooling anthropologists for over 40 years. In 1912, fossils found in England were hailed as the "missing link" between apes and humans. It wasn't until 1953 that tests revealed the skull was a mix of human and orangutan bones, deliberately stained to look ancient.

◎ In 1726, Mary Toft convinced doctors she was giving birth to rabbits. She had actually been inserting rabbit parts into herself before labor, fooling even the king's physicians. When the truth came out, she was imprisoned for fraud, but the bizarre case left England questioning medical science for years.

◎ In the 1960s, an Italian prankster convinced wine lovers that he had discovered the "Fountain of Bacchus," a natural spring flowing with endless red wine. The truth? He had simply rigged a pipe from a nearby winery. Tourists flocked to taste the miracle—until they noticed the faint scent of fermentation tanks nearby.

◎ The "Shroud of Turin," believed to be Jesus Christ's burial cloth, has been the subject of intense debate for centuries. Carbon dating tests in 1988 revealed it was actually created in the 14th century, over a thousand years after Jesus lived. Despite this, many still believe in its authenticity.

◎ In 1971, BBC aired a documentary exposing the existence of the "Spaghetti Tree" in Switzerland, showing farmers harvesting pasta from tree branches. Many viewers, unaware it was an April Fool's joke, called in asking how they could grow their own spaghetti trees at home. The BBC had to explain that spaghetti does not, in fact, grow on trees.

◎ The Loch Ness Monster became a worldwide phenomenon in 1934 after a famous photo showed a long-necked creature emerging from the water. Decades later, it was revealed that the "monster" was a toy submarine with a sculpted head, placed in the water as a prank. Despite this, people still flock to Loch Ness in hopes of spotting Nessie.

◎ The "Hitler Diaries" scandal rocked the 1980s when a German magazine paid millions for what they believed were Adolf Hitler's personal journals. The handwriting expert vouched for their authenticity—until forensic tests proved they were modern forgeries. The forger, Konrad Kujau, later admitted he had used cheap school notebooks to create them.

◎ In the 1960s, a man named Gray Barker helped spread the legend of the "Men in Black" by fabricating stories of mysterious agents silencing UFO witnesses. His books and claims inspired countless conspiracy theories. Ironically, his letters later revealed he had made most of it up for fun and profit.

◎ In 1865, a con artist named William Mumler convinced people he could photograph spirits. His "ghost photos" were actually double exposures, often using old images of the deceased. Even P.T. Barnum exposed him as a fraud, but not before grieving families paid small fortunes for ghostly keepsakes.

◎ The 1967 Patterson-Gimlin film, supposedly showing Bigfoot walking through a California forest, remains one of the most famous cryptid sightings. Though many believe it's real, skeptics argue that it was just a man in a gorilla suit. Even one of the film's crew members later admitted it was staged.

◎ In 1930, a fake archeological discovery in Mexico claimed to unearth an ancient Mayan spaceship. The artifact, covered in strange symbols, turned out to be a modern carving made with metal tools. Despite being debunked, the story continues to appear in alien conspiracy circles.

◎ The 1999 "Blair Witch Project" movie convinced many that its found-footage horror was real. The filmmakers even created a fake website and news stories to build the illusion. The campaign was so effective that some fans went searching for the fictional Blair Witch in the Maryland woods.

◎ In 1957, the Tasaday tribe in the Philippines was hailed as a "Stone Age" people who had never contacted modern civilization. Years later, journalists discovered they had been staged by the government, with participants wearing costumes and pretending to live primitively. The elaborate ruse was meant to attract tourism and funding.

◎ In the 1890s, a group of pranksters started a rumor that Kentucky's bluegrass got its color from being watered with copper-infused moonshine. The myth spread so widely that some farmers actually started experimenting with copper sulfate. The grass remained green.

◎ A 1969 magazine article claimed that NASA spent millions developing a pen that could write in space while the Soviets simply used a pencil. In reality, both NASA and the USSR used pencils until an independent inventor created the "Space Pen" and sold it to both space programs.

◎ The "Bathtub Hoax" of 1917 claimed that President Millard Fillmore installed the first bathtub in the White House. Newspapers ran the story as fact, but it was completely made up by journalist H.L. Mencken. Despite his later confession, the myth persists in some history books today.

◎ In 1864, a fossilized giant human skeleton was "discovered" in France, supposedly proving the existence of prehistoric giants. The skeleton was actually a carefully sculpted hoax made of plaster. The prank was meant to mock gullible scientists, but some still cite it as evidence of giants.

◎ The "Tupac is Alive" theory gained traction after multiple posthumous albums and supposed sightings of the rapper in Cuba. One of the biggest fuelers of the hoax was his own record label, which released music videos featuring cryptic clues suggesting he faked his death. Despite no real evidence, some fans still believe.

◎ A fake 2001 story claimed that Microsoft had purchased the Catholic Church and would start offering online confessions. The hoax email spread rapidly, forcing Microsoft to issue an official denial. Some people still reference it as an example of tech companies controlling everything.

◎ The "Montauk Project" hoax claims that the U.S. military experimented with time travel and mind control on Long Island. While the story has no proof, it inspired the hit show *Stranger Things*. The alleged whistleblower who started the rumors later admitted he had a vivid imagination.

◎ The Lying Stones of Dr. Beringer were a set of fake fossils carved with biblical imagery and sold as divine evidence in the 1700s. The hoax was exposed when one fossil was found with Beringer's own name carved onto it. Humiliated, he spent his life trying to erase the scandal from history.

◎ In 1996, Taco Bell ran a fake ad claiming they had purchased the Liberty Bell and renamed it the "Taco Liberty Bell." Outraged citizens flooded the National Park Service with complaints—until Taco Bell admitted it was an April Fool's prank. Sales skyrocketed anyway.

UNSOLVED MYSTERIES

⊚ The Dyatlov Pass Incident is one of the most chilling unsolved mysteries. In 1959, nine experienced hikers were found dead in the Russian wilderness, some with crushed skulls, others missing body parts, and their tent bizarrely cut from the inside. Theories range from secret military tests to infrasound-induced panic, but no explanation fully accounts for the strange details.

⊚ The Voynich Manuscript remains one of history's most cryptic books. Written in an unknown language with bizarre illustrations of plants that don't exist, it has defied codebreakers for centuries. Even experts in linguistics, cryptography, and AI have failed to crack its meaning.

⊚ The Dancing Plague of 1518 saw hundreds of people in Strasbourg, France, dance uncontrollably for weeks. Many collapsed from exhaustion, and some even died. To this day, historians debate whether it was caused by mass hysteria, a fungal toxin, or an unknown neurological disorder.

⊚ The Taos Hum is a low-frequency sound heard by only a small percentage of people in Taos, New Mexico. Described as a persistent droning noise, scientists have never pinpointed its source. Some suspect industrial activity, while others believe it's caused by an unexplained natural phenomenon.

⊚ The Zodiac Killer's identity remains unknown, despite his taunting ciphers and letters to the media in the 1960s and '70s. In 2020, a team of cryptographers cracked one of his complex ciphers, but his true identity is still a mystery. Several suspects have been proposed, but none conclusively match the evidence.

⊚ The Wow! Signal, detected in 1977, was a powerful 72-second radio burst from deep space that has never been explained. It was so unusual that astronomer Jerry Ehman circled it on the printout and wrote "Wow!" beside it. Despite decades of searching, no similar signal has ever been detected.

⊚ The Mary Celeste was discovered adrift in the Atlantic in 1872 with no one aboard. The ship was undamaged, its cargo intact, and the crew's belongings untouched. There were no signs of struggle, and the crew was never seen again.

⊚ The Somerton Man case, also known as the Tamam Shud mystery, is one of Australia's strangest unsolved deaths. A well-dressed man was found dead on an Adelaide beach in 1948 with no ID, missing labels from his clothing, and a cryptic note reading "Tamam Shud" (Persian for "it is finished"). Despite decades of investigation, his identity remains unknown.

⊚ The Oak Island Money Pit has baffled treasure hunters for over 200 years. A deep, booby-trapped shaft on Oak Island, Nova Scotia, is rumored to contain hidden treasure—possibly linked to the Knights Templar. Despite millions of dollars spent digging, the true contents remain undiscovered.

⊚ The Green Children of Woolpit were two children who appeared in 12th-century England, speaking an unknown language and with green-tinged skin. They eventually adapted to normal food, and their skin color faded, but their origins remain a mystery. Some theories suggest they were lost children from an underground world or suffered from a rare medical condition.

⊚ The Devil's Footprints appeared in England in 1855 after a night of heavy snowfall. A trail of hoof-like prints stretched for miles, crossing rooftops and high walls. No one ever determined what made them, with theories ranging from strange animals to supernatural forces.

◎ The Black Dahlia murder is one of Hollywood's most infamous unsolved crimes. In 1947, aspiring actress Elizabeth Short was found brutally murdered, her body bisected and drained of blood. Despite numerous theories and suspects, her killer was never caught.

◎ The Flannan Isles lighthouse mystery occurred in 1900 when three lighthouse keepers vanished without a trace. Their last log entries describe a terrible storm—but weather records show there was no storm at the time. No bodies were ever found, and the case remains open.

◎ The Vanishing of the Sodder Children is a chilling missing persons case from 1945. A house fire supposedly killed five children, but no remains were ever found. Decades later, strange sightings and anonymous letters suggested they might have been kidnapped.

◎ The Hollinwell Incident saw over 300 children collapse simultaneously at a school event in England in 1980. No toxins or gas leaks were found, and many victims reported dizziness and nausea before losing consciousness. The cause remains unknown.

◎ The Tunguska Event of 1908 flattened 800 square miles of Siberian forest, but no impact crater was ever found. Scientists believe it was caused by an exploding asteroid or comet, but no fragments have ever been recovered. The explosion released energy equivalent to more than 1,000 Hiroshima bombs.

◎ The Man from Taured is a legend of a traveler who allegedly arrived at a Japanese airport with a passport from a country that doesn't exist. Authorities were baffled, and when he was placed in a hotel under surveillance, he vanished without a trace. No records of him were ever found.

◎ The Hinterkaifeck Murders remain one of Germany's creepiest mysteries. In 1922, an entire family was brutally murdered on their remote farmstead. Days before the attack, the father reported hearing footsteps in the attic, but no culprit was ever found.

⊚ The Max Headroom Broadcast Intrusion happened in 1987 when an unknown hacker interrupted Chicago TV stations with a bizarre video of a masked figure in a wobbly Max Headroom mask. The signal hijack lasted only minutes, and the perpetrators were never identified.

⊚ The Lead Masks Case involved two Brazilian men found dead on a hilltop in 1966. They were wearing lead masks and had notes mentioning an "energetic test." No cause of death was ever determined, and their motives remain unknown.

⊚ The Phantom Cosmonaut theory suggests that Soviet astronauts died in space before Yuri Gagarin's historic flight in 1961. Alleged recordings of dying cosmonauts and Soviet secrecy fuel speculation that there were earlier, hidden spaceflight disasters.

⊚ The Isdal Woman was found dead in Norway in 1970 under bizarre circumstances. She carried multiple passports, wore disguises, and had her labels removed from clothing. Her cause of death was ruled a probable suicide, but many believe she was a spy.

⊚ The Stonehenge mystery persists, as archaeologists still debate how ancient builders moved the massive stones. Some are from over 150 miles away, requiring transportation methods that remain unexplained. The site's exact purpose is also still unknown.

⊚ The Loch Ness Monster remains one of the world's most famous cryptids. Though many photos have been debunked, sonar readings and eyewitness accounts continue to fuel speculation. Some believe Nessie is a surviving prehistoric creature, while others suggest a hoax or natural misidentification.

⊚ The Tungsten Treasure of Georgia refers to a buried hoard of tungsten bars worth millions, supposedly hidden during WWII. Despite treasure hunters scouring the area, it has never been found. Some believe it was moved before it could be recovered.

⊚ The Curse of King Tut's Tomb gained notoriety when several people involved in its discovery died under mysterious circumstances. While many deaths were later explained, the legend of the curse persists. Some say the tomb's air contained ancient mold that made explorers sick.

◎ Legend has it that a remote village in Canada vanished without a trace. In 1930, the entire population of Lake Anjikuni, a small Inuit settlement, reportedly disappeared overnight, leaving food on tables and fires still burning. No bodies were ever found, and the mystery remains one of Canada's most chilling legends.

LINGUISTIC CURIOSITIES

◎ The English word "alphabet" comes from the first two letters of the Greek alphabet, alpha and beta. Many ancient scripts followed a similar naming convention, but English is one of the few modern languages that retains the reference.

◎ The longest word in the English language is a 189,819-letter chemical name for the protein titin. It would take over three hours to say aloud, so most dictionaries don't even bother including it.

◎ The dot above the letters "i" and "j" has a name—it's called a *tittle*. The word comes from Latin and originally meant a small stroke or accent in writing.

◎ The phrase "it's all Greek to me" isn't unique to English. In Greek, they say, "It's Chinese to me," while in Chinese, they say, "It's like Martian speech." Many cultures assume the hardest language is spoken somewhere else.

◎ The Cherokee syllabary, created by Sequoyah in the early 1800s, was one of the only known cases of a writing system being invented by a single person. Despite never having learned to read or write himself, he designed a fully functional script still used today.

◎ The word "girl" originally had no connection to gender. In Middle English, it simply meant "a young person" and could refer to boys or girls alike.

◎ Shakespeare introduced over 1,700 words, including "bedazzled," "obscene,", "cold-blooded," "lonely," "swagger," and even "eyeball." He often tweaked existing words, mashed others together, or borrowed from different languages.

◎ The only letter that doesn't appear in any U.S. state name is "Q." Even tricky letters like X (Texas), Z (Arizona), and J (New Jersey) manage to make an appearance.

◎ The most translated book in the world is the Bible, but the second most translated is *The Little Prince* by Antoine de Saint-Exupéry. It has been published in over 500 languages, including some rare dialects with only a few hundred speakers.

◎ In French, the number 80 is "quatre-vingts," which literally means "four twenties." This counting system, called "vigesimal," likely comes from an ancient Celtic influence where people counted in groups of 20 instead of 10.

◎ The longest palindromic word in English is "tattarrattat," coined by James Joyce in *Ulysses* to imitate the sound of knocking on a door. It reads the same forward and backward, making it a perfect literary knock-knock joke.

◎ There's a language spoken by whistling. The "Silbo Gomero" language of the Canary Islands replaces words with whistles that can carry over long distances, helping farmers communicate across valleys.

◎ The letter "E" is the most common in English, appearing in about 11% of all words. This is why lipograms—texts that deliberately avoid a specific letter—often challenge writers to omit "E," the most frequently used letter in the language.

◎ The Hawaiian alphabet only has 13 letters: five vowels and eight consonants. This is why so many Hawaiian words have repeating sounds, like "aloha" and "Hawaii."

◎ Some languages don't distinguish between blue and green. In Vietnamese, the word *xanh* covers both colors, with additional descriptors added only when necessary.

◎ The word "salary" comes from the Latin *salarium*, which referred to the money Roman soldiers were paid to buy salt. At one point in history, salt was so valuable that it was used as currency.

◎ The English word "clue" originally meant a ball of yarn or thread. It comes from Greek mythology, where Theseus used a string (a *clew*) to navigate the labyrinth and escape the Minotaur.

◎ The longest word in major dictionaries is "pneumonoultramicroscopicsilicovolcanoconiosis." It was created as a joke in the 1930s but still describes a real lung disease caused by inhaling fine silica dust.

◎ The Pirahã language, spoken by an Amazonian tribe, has no words for specific numbers. Instead, they use terms like "few" and "many," making it one of the only known languages without numerical counting.

◎ English is the only major language where "I" is always capitalized. Most other languages, including French and Spanish, keep their first-person pronouns lowercase unless at the start of a sentence.

◎ The word "goodbye" originally came from the phrase "God be with ye." Over time, the words blended together into a single expression of farewell.

◎ Japanese has a word, *tsundoku*, for the habit of buying books and letting them pile up without reading them. There is no direct English equivalent, though many book lovers can relate.

◎ The word "barbarian" originally came from ancient Greece, where it was used to describe anyone who didn't speak Greek. To them, foreign languages sounded like "bar-bar-bar"—a noise rather than speech.

◎ The longest word ever published comes from a 19th-century Sanskrit dictionary. At 195 characters, it's a compound word describing a region in India and is impossible to pronounce without stopping for breath.

◎ The term "bug" for a computer glitch dates back to Thomas Edison, but it became famous when a real moth was found stuck in an early computer's hardware. Engineers removed it and literally "debugged" the system.

◎ The word "alphabet" isn't just for letters. It's been borrowed into many fields, including the world of animals, where it describes the pecking order of social groups—hence "alpha male" and "beta wolf."

◎ There are over 7,000 languages spoken in the world today, but more than half of the population speaks just 23 of them. Meanwhile, nearly 40% of languages have fewer than 1,000 speakers and are at risk of extinction.

◎ The most widely spoken language is English, but the language with the most native speakers is Mandarin Chinese, with over 920 million people using it as their first language.

◎ The sentence "The quick brown fox jumps over the lazy dog" contains every letter of the English alphabet. This type of sentence is called a pangram and is used for typing practice and font testing.

◎ Basque, spoken in Spain and France, is a linguistic mystery. It has no known connection to any other language and is believed to predate the arrival of Indo-European languages in Europe.

◎ Icelandic has remained almost unchanged for centuries, meaning modern Icelanders can still read medieval sagas with little difficulty. Meanwhile, English speakers would struggle to understand Old English from just 1,000 years ago.

◎ More people in Africa speak French than in France. Countries like the Democratic Republic of Congo, Ivory Coast, and Senegal have millions of native and second-language French speakers.

◎ The Hawaiian language was once nearly extinct, with fewer than 50 native speakers left in the 1980s. Thanks to revitalization efforts, the number has now grown into the thousands.

◎ Inuktitut, the language spoken by Indigenous people in Canada, has over 50 words to describe different types of snow, based on its texture, shape, and interaction with the environment. However, Scotland surpasses that with an astonishing 421 words for snow.

◎ In Japanese, there are different levels of politeness, and the way you speak depends on whom you're addressing. Using the wrong level of politeness can make you sound rude or overly formal.

◎ Sign languages are not universal—each country (and sometimes regions within a country) has its own distinct sign language. American Sign Language (ASL) is more closely related to French Sign Language than to British Sign Language.

◎ The shortest sentence in English is "I am." It's a complete sentence with a subject and a verb, making it one of the simplest yet grammatically correct statements.

◎ Papua New Guinea has the highest linguistic diversity in the world, with over 800 languages spoken. Many of these languages have fewer than 1,000 speakers, making them highly endangered.

◎ There is a language spoken in Mexico called Ayapaneco that nearly went extinct because its last two fluent speakers refused to talk to each other.

◎ The longest place name in the world belongs to a hill in New Zealand: *Taumatawhakatangihangakoauauotamateaturipukakapikimaungahoronukupokaiwhenuakitanatahu.* Locals usually just call it "Taumata."

◎ The Yuchi language, spoken by a Native American tribe, is unrelated to any other known language in the world. It is classified as a language isolate, meaning it has no linguistic relatives.

◎ Welsh nearly vanished in the 20th century, but thanks to government protection and education programs, it is now growing again, with bilingual road signs and mandatory language classes in schools.

◎ Some languages, like Rotokas (spoken in Papua New Guinea), have as few as 12 letters in their alphabet, while others, like Khmer (spoken in Cambodia), have over 70.

◎ The word "quiz" allegedly came from a Dublin theater owner who bet he could invent a word and make it widely used in a single day. He wrote "quiz" on walls across the city, and by the next morning, everyone was talking about it.

◎ The Eskimo-Aleut languages have different words for "you" based on how many people are being addressed. There is a separate pronoun for talking to one person, two people, or three or more people.

THE U.S. POSTAL SERVICE

◎ The United States Postal Service (USPS) is older than the country itself. It was established in 1775 by the Second Continental Congress, with Benjamin Franklin as the first Postmaster General.

◎ The famous motto of the USPS—"Neither snow nor rain nor heat nor gloom of night stays these couriers from the swift completion of their appointed rounds"—isn't actually its official motto. It comes from an inscription on the New York City General Post Office, inspired by ancient Persian couriers.

◎ In 1913, when the Parcel Post service began, some parents mailed their children because it was cheaper than buying a train ticket. The USPS quickly banned this after a few cases made headlines.

◎ The Pony Express lasted only 18 months before the transcontinental telegraph made it obsolete. Despite its legendary status, it was a financial disaster and was never run by the USPS.

◎ The first U.S. postage stamp was issued in 1847 and featured Benjamin Franklin, honoring his role as the first Postmaster General.

◎ The Postal Service delivers to the bottom of the Grand Canyon using mule trains. Supai, Arizona, is one of the most remote towns in the country and still relies on this old-fashioned delivery method.

◎ The USPS handles nearly half of the world's mail. It processes about 425 million pieces of mail every day—more than 150 billion annually.

◎ In 1987, a postal worker in Utah successfully mailed himself from Los Angeles to Salt Lake City inside a wooden crate. He survived the journey, but the USPS was not amused.

◎ ZIP codes were introduced in 1963 to improve mail sorting efficiency. The term "ZIP" stands for "Zone Improvement Plan," and the system was heavily promoted with the help of a cartoon character named "Mr. ZIP."

◎ The most unusual postal route in the U.S. is in the Florida Keys, where a mail carrier delivers mail by boat to people living on isolated islands.

◎ The USPS has its own police force, the Postal Inspection Service, which is one of the oldest federal law enforcement agencies in the country. Its agents investigate mail fraud, theft, and even cybercrimes.

◎ Every year, the USPS receives thousands of letters addressed to Santa Claus. The "Operation Santa" program allows volunteers to respond to children's letters and even fulfill some of their Christmas wishes.

◎ The only floating post office in the U.S. is the J.W. Westcott II in Detroit, Michigan. It delivers mail to passing ships while they're still moving.

◎ Dogs attacking mail carriers is such a frequent problem that the USPS keeps an annual list of the cities with the most dog bites. Postal workers collectively suffer thousands of dog attacks each year.

◎ The USPS has a secret recovery unit known as the "Mail Recovery Center" (formerly the Dead Letter Office). It handles undeliverable mail and even auctions off unclaimed items.

◎ Postage stamps weren't required in the early days of mail service. Instead, the recipient had to pay upon delivery, leading to many people refusing their letters to avoid the fee.

◎ The longest rural delivery route in the U.S. covers over 180 miles. A single carrier in rural Oklahoma makes the journey every day to serve just a handful of customers.

◎ The shortest postal route in the country is in Philadelphia, Pennsylvania, covering just a few city blocks.

◎ The U.S. Postal Service briefly experimented with missile mail. In 1959, a Navy submarine launched a guided missile carrying 3,000 letters, proving that mail could be delivered in minutes—but the idea never took off.

◎ The White House has its own private post office, but it doesn't deliver mail directly to the President. All letters go through security screening before reaching the Oval Office.

◎ The post office once issued stamps made from actual silk and steel. These limited-edition stamps were part of a series showcasing American industry.

◎ The most expensive U.S. postage stamp ever sold was a rare 1918 "Inverted Jenny," which featured an upside-down airplane. One of these misprints was auctioned for $1.6 million in 2018.

◎ The USPS was the first government agency to hire women during wartime. Women worked as mail carriers and clerks during the Civil War when men left for battle.

◎ Originally called Hot Springs, Truth or Consequences, New Mexico, changed its name in 1950 after winning a radio contest hosted by the radio show, *Truth or Consequences*. The town voted for the change, and the post office updated all records to match.

◎ Owney, a stray dog, became the unofficial mascot of the Railway Mail Service in the 1890s. He traveled the country on mail trains and even received a collection of tags and medals for his journeys.

◎ The first airmail service in the U.S. started in 1918 and was flown between Washington, D.C., Philadelphia, and New York City. Pilots often had to navigate using roadmaps because aviation technology was still primitive.

◎ There's a post office inside a volcano. The world's only underwater post office operates in Vanuatu, where snorkelers can mail waterproof postcards from beneath the ocean.

◎ Mail carriers used to deliver letters multiple times a day in large cities. In the 1800s, some areas had up to seven daily deliveries.

◎ The U.S. Postal Service owns one of the largest civilian vehicle fleets in the world, with over 230,000 trucks and vans delivering mail to every corner of the country.

◎ During the Cold War, the USPS developed a "Doomsday Mail System" to ensure letters could still be delivered in case of a nuclear attack. Luckily, it never had to be used.

◎ The Grumman Long Life Vehicle (LLV) has been the backbone of the U.S. Postal Service fleet since the 1980s. Built to last just 24 years, many are still in service nearly 40 years later, despite lacking air conditioning and modern safety features. Their distinctive boxy design and right-hand drive make them instantly recognizable on American streets.

⊚ A burglar was once caught because he took a bite out of a piece of cheese at the crime scene. Investigators matched his dental impression to the bite mark on the cheese, proving his guilt.

⊚ The first case ever solved using fingerprint evidence was in Argentina in 1892. A woman named Francisca Rojas falsely accused a neighbor of murdering her two children, but investigators found her bloody fingerprint at the crime scene—proving she was the killer.

⊚ DNA evidence has solved crimes decades after they were committed, but it has also led to false convictions. In one case, a man was wrongly charged with murder because his DNA was found at the scene—later, it was discovered he had been transported in the same ambulance as the victim months earlier.

⊚ The FBI maintains a database called CODIS (Combined DNA Index System), which contains millions of DNA profiles. In some cases, criminals were caught because their relatives were in the system, allowing investigators to track them through family connections.

⊚ Bite mark analysis was once considered strong forensic evidence, but it has led to multiple wrongful convictions. Studies have shown that human bite marks are not as unique as fingerprints, and skin is too elastic to preserve an accurate impression.

⊚ The famous crime-solving technique of matching bullets to a gun, called ballistic fingerprinting, is not always foolproof. Some criminals alter their gun barrels after committing a crime, changing the unique markings that would normally link a bullet to the weapon.

⊚ In the 1930s, a forensic scientist named Frances Glessner Lee created incredibly detailed crime scene dioramas called the "Nutshell Studies of Unexplained Death." These miniature models were used to train homicide detectives and are still studied today.

⊚ The FBI once caught a bank robber by analyzing the glitter left at the crime scene. The tiny reflective particles matched the type of glitter in the suspect's craft supplies, leading to his arrest.

⊚ In 1994, police solved a cold case by analyzing tree DNA. A woman's body was found near a palo verde tree, and forensic botanists matched seed pods from the crime scene to the tree in the suspect's truck, proving he had been there.

⊚ The world's first police crime lab was established in France in 1910 by Edmond Locard, the founder of modern forensic science. His principle, "Every contact leaves a trace," became the foundation of crime scene investigation.

⊚ A criminal was once caught because of a mosquito. Investigators found a blood-filled mosquito in his apartment and tested the DNA, confirming it matched the victim.

⊚ Some forensic artists can reconstruct a person's face based only on their skull. This technique, called forensic facial reconstruction, has helped identify unknown murder victims years or even decades after their deaths.

⊚ In one of the earliest forensic cases, a Chinese investigator in the 1200s solved a murder by having all the villagers lay out their sickles in the sun. Flies swarmed to one particular sickle, which had invisible traces of blood, identifying the killer.

◎ Gait analysis, or studying the way a person walks, has been used to solve crimes. In one case, British investigators identified a suspect from blurry CCTV footage by analyzing his distinctive limp.

◎ Lipstick smudges have been used to solve crimes. Forensic scientists have developed a technique to analyze lipstick residue on glasses, tissues, or even skin to identify the brand and match it to a suspect.

◎ Handwriting analysis can reveal more than just the identity of a writer. Experts have solved crimes by detecting hidden messages in ransom notes, identifying disguised handwriting, or recognizing signs of mental distress in a suspect's writing.

◎ In 2008, a man was convicted of arson after forensic experts analyzed the pattern of burn marks on his clothes. The fire-resistant lining of his jacket had melted in a way that indicated he had been exposed to extreme heat at close range.

◎ Ear print evidence has been used to solve burglaries. Some criminals press their ears against doors or windows to listen before breaking in, leaving a unique ear impression behind.

◎ The "Smiling Bandit" was caught because of the way he held his gun. Witnesses described his unique grip, which matched how he held a firearm in old photos, leading to his identification and arrest.

◎ In 2012, a hit-and-run suspect was caught because a tiny piece of their car's headlight was found at the crime scene. Investigators traced the fragment to a specific make and model, which led them to the driver.

◎ In 1986, the first-ever case solved using DNA evidence happened in England. A man named Colin Pitchfork was identified as a murderer after police conducted mass DNA testing, a method now used worldwide.

◎ In a bizarre case, a murder was solved because of the bacteria in the victim's body. Scientists identified a rare strain of bacteria in her bloodstream, which was traced back to water contamination at the suspect's house.

◎ In 2003, police used pollen analysis to solve a crime. They found microscopic pollen grains on a suspect's clothing, which matched a rare plant species found only at the crime scene.

◎ Some forensic labs analyze the way clothes absorb water to determine how long a body has been submerged. This technique has helped solve drowning cases and pinpoint time of death.

◎ In one case, a dog's paw print led to a murder conviction. The victim's dog had stepped in the suspect's blood, and the paw print pattern helped investigators reconstruct the sequence of events.

◎ A criminal was once identified because of the way he tied knots. Investigators compared the complex knots used in a kidnapping to the suspect's history as a sailor, leading to his arrest.

◎ Computer forensic experts can retrieve deleted emails, texts, and even files that were intentionally wiped. This method has been crucial in solving fraud cases, cybercrimes, and even homicides.

◎ In the 1990s, an arsonist was caught because of the chemical composition of the matchsticks he used. The match heads contained a unique formula only used in one factory, which led police to a suspect.

SCANDALS

◎ The 1919 Black Sox scandal involved eight Chicago White Sox players accused of intentionally losing the World Series in exchange for bribes from gamblers. Although they were acquitted in court, they were banned from baseball for life.

◎ The Watergate scandal, which led to President Richard Nixon's resignation in 1974, started with a seemingly minor burglary at the Democratic National Committee headquarters. The cover-up was worse than the crime—tapes revealed Nixon's involvement, and he resigned before he could be impeached.

◎ The Teapot Dome scandal in the 1920s was one of the biggest political corruption cases in U.S. history. Government officials secretly leased oil reserves to private companies in exchange for bribes, and it was the first time a U.S. cabinet member was sent to prison.

◎ The Enron scandal of 2001 was a corporate fraud disaster. The company used shady accounting tricks to hide debt and inflate profits, leading to one of the largest bankruptcies in history and the downfall of accounting giant Arthur Andersen.

◎ The Iran-Contra affair in the 1980s exposed a secret U.S. operation where weapons were sold to Iran, and the profits were used to fund

Nicaraguan rebels. President Ronald Reagan denied knowledge of the scheme, but documents suggested otherwise.

◎ The Volkswagen emissions scandal of 2015 revealed that the company had installed software to cheat emissions tests. Their cars were producing up to 40 times the legal limit of pollutants, leading to billions in fines and a massive recall.

◎ The "Quiz Show Scandal" of the 1950s uncovered that game shows were rigged. Contestants were fed answers to boost ratings, and the controversy led to new laws preventing televised fraud.

◎ The College Admissions Scandal of 2019, known as "Operation Varsity Blues," revealed that wealthy parents, including celebrities, paid bribes to get their kids into elite universities. The scam involved fake athletic credentials and SAT test cheating.

◎ The "Pentagon Papers" scandal in 1971 exposed government deception about the Vietnam War. Daniel Ellsberg leaked classified documents showing that officials had lied to the public about U.S. progress in the war.

◎ The Ford Pinto scandal of the 1970s revealed that the car had a dangerously placed fuel tank prone to exploding in rear-end collisions. Ford knew about the defect but calculated it was cheaper to pay lawsuits than to fix the issue.

◎ The FIFA corruption scandal of 2015 uncovered widespread bribery and vote-rigging in the world's governing soccer organization. Top officials were accused of taking millions in kickbacks to award World Cup hosting rights.

◎ The Duke lacrosse scandal of 2006 was a case of false accusation. Three members of the Duke University lacrosse team were charged with assault, but the case collapsed after it was revealed that the prosecutor had withheld evidence.

◎ Lance Armstrong's doping scandal rocked the sports world. After years of denying allegations, the seven-time Tour de France winner admitted to using performance-enhancing drugs, leading to his lifetime ban from cycling.

◎ The Theranos scandal exposed a Silicon Valley fraud. CEO Elizabeth Holmes claimed her company had developed revolutionary blood-testing technology, but it was a complete fraud—her devices never worked.

◎ The Chappaquiddick incident in 1969 involved Senator Ted Kennedy driving off a bridge, resulting in the drowning of passenger Mary Jo Kopechne. Kennedy left the scene and waited hours to report the accident, damaging his political career permanently.

◎ The Bernie Madoff Ponzi scheme was the largest financial fraud in history. Madoff ran a $65 billion investment scam, paying old investors with new money until the scheme collapsed in 2008.

◎ The Love Canal environmental disaster of the 1970s revealed that a neighborhood in New York was built on a toxic waste dump. Residents suffered severe health problems, leading to a national reckoning over corporate environmental negligence.

◎ The News of the World phone hacking scandal in 2011 exposed that journalists were illegally accessing voicemails of celebrities, politicians, and crime victims. The scandal led to the closure of the 168-year-old newspaper and criminal convictions.

◎ The Catholic Church sexual abuse scandal, exposed in the early 2000s, revealed decades of systematic child abuse cover-ups. The scandal led to lawsuits, resignations, and major changes in church policies worldwide.

◎ The Credit Mobilier scandal of the 1870s involved railroad companies overcharging the U.S. government for construction. Politicians were bribed to keep quiet, and the scandal reached the highest levels of government.

◎ The 2002 Salt Lake City Olympics bribery scandal revealed that members of the International Olympic Committee had been bribed to award the games to Utah. The scandal led to reforms in how cities bid for the Olympics.

- The Bill Clinton-Monica Lewinsky scandal resulted in only the second impeachment of a U.S. president. Clinton was acquitted in the Senate, but the scandal dominated headlines for years.

- The Operation ABSCAM sting of the late 1970s caught U.S. politicians accepting bribes from FBI agents posing as Arab businessmen. Several congressmen were convicted in the high-profile corruption case.

- The Jack Abramoff lobbying scandal in the 2000s exposed a massive web of bribery, fraud, and corruption involving politicians, casinos, and Native American tribes. Abramoff served prison time for his role in the scheme.

- The Horse Meat Scandal of 2013 revealed that some European beef products actually contained horse meat. Major food brands were caught in the scandal, leading to recalls and public outrage.

- The Boeing 737 MAX scandal exposed that the company rushed production of a new aircraft and ignored safety concerns. Two deadly crashes killed hundreds, and investigations revealed Boeing had misled regulators.

- The John Edwards scandal revealed that the former U.S. senator and presidential candidate had an affair and fathered a child while his wife was battling cancer. He was later indicted for misusing campaign funds to cover it up.

- The Equifax data breach of 2017 exposed personal information of 147 million Americans. The credit reporting company failed to fix a security flaw, allowing hackers to steal sensitive data like Social Security numbers.

- The Panama Papers leak in 2016 exposed secret offshore accounts of politicians, celebrities, and billionaires. The leaked documents revealed how the wealthy hid their money to avoid taxes.

BASEBALL

⚙ The longest professional baseball game lasted 33 innings and took over eight hours to complete. The Pawtucket Red Sox and the Rochester Red Wings battled from April 18-19, 1981, before the game was paused at 4:09 a.m. and finished two months later.

⚙ The fastest pitch ever recorded in Major League Baseball was thrown by Aroldis Chapman in 2010. His fastball clocked in at 105.8 mph, making it nearly impossible for batters to react in time.

⚙ Babe Ruth once hit a home run out of Forbes Field that landed in a passing car. The driver reportedly kept the ball as a souvenir.

⚙ Before Jackie Robinson broke baseball's color barrier in 1947, an African American player named Moses Fleetwood Walker played in the major leagues in 1884. However, after his short career, baseball became segregated for over 60 years.

⚙ The Chicago Cubs went 108 years without winning a World Series, the longest championship drought in professional sports history. They finally broke the "Curse of the Billy Goat" in 2016.

⚙ A baseball used in an MLB game lasts an average of only six pitches before being replaced. Teams go through roughly 120 baseballs per game, adding up to over 900,000 used in a single season.

◎ The only no-hitter in a World Series game was thrown by Don Larsen of the New York Yankees in 1956. Even more impressive, it was a perfect game—meaning no batter reached base at all.

◎ The shortest player in MLB history was Eddie Gaedel, who stood just 3 feet 7 inches tall. The St. Louis Browns signed him for a publicity stunt in 1951, and he walked on four pitches because his strike zone was almost nonexistent.

◎ The baseball Hall of Fame is located in Cooperstown, New York, but the idea that baseball was invented there is a myth. The game evolved from earlier bat-and-ball sports, with no single inventor.

◎ Cal Ripken Jr. holds the record for the longest consecutive games played streak, appearing in 2,632 straight games over 16 years. His durability earned him the nickname "The Iron Man" of baseball.

◎ Baseballs are hand-stitched with exactly 108 double stitches. The red thread stands out against the white leather, making it easier for batters to see the spin of the ball.

◎ The New York Yankees have won more World Series titles than any other team. As of 2024, they have claimed 27 championships, making them the most successful franchise in MLB history.

◎ The average MLB player has just 0.4 seconds to react to a 95 mph fastball. That's faster than the blink of an eye, requiring incredible reflexes and split-second decision-making.

◎ The first World Series was played in 1903 between the Boston Americans (now Red Sox) and the Pittsburgh Pirates. Boston won the best-of-nine series, five games to three.

◎ In 1974, Atlanta Braves player Hank Aaron broke Babe Ruth's long-standing home run record by hitting his 715th career homer. He finished with 755, a record that stood until Barry Bonds surpassed it in 2007.

◎ The longest home run ever recorded in MLB was hit by Mickey Mantle in 1953. It traveled an estimated 565 feet, though unofficial reports suggest even longer distances for some of his other legendary blasts.

◎ The Boston Red Sox famously traded Babe Ruth to the New York Yankees in 1919, which many believe started the "Curse of the Bambino." The Red Sox didn't win another World Series for 86 years.

◎ The Pittsburgh Pirates were the first MLB team to wear uniform numbers on their jerseys full-time, starting in 1932. Before that, players were often identified by position rather than number.

◎ The highest-scoring game in MLB history was a 1922 matchup between the Chicago Cubs and Philadelphia Phillies. The Cubs won 26-23, with a total of 49 runs scored between both teams.

◎ The Los Angeles Dodgers were originally based in Brooklyn and were known as the "Trolley Dodgers," a reference to New Yorkers dodging streetcars in the early 1900s.

◎ Hall of Fame pitcher Nolan Ryan threw a record seven no-hitters in his career. No other pitcher has thrown more than four.

◎ The first night game in MLB history was played on May 24, 1935, at Cincinnati's Crosley Field. Before stadium lights, all games had to be played during the day.

◎ Baseball was once an Olympic sport, but it was removed after the 2008 Games. However, it made a return for the Tokyo 2020 Olympics before being dropped again for Paris 2024.

◎ The oldest professional baseball stadium still in use is Fenway Park in Boston. Built in 1912, it's famous for its quirky dimensions, including the towering "Green Monster" in left field.

◎ The lowest recorded attendance for an MLB game was on April 29, 2015, when the Baltimore Orioles played in an empty stadium due to citywide unrest after the death of Freddie Gray in police custody. With a curfew in place and safety concerns high, MLB barred fans, making it the first game in history with an official attendance of zero.

◎ The slowest pitch ever recorded for a strike in an MLB game was 31 mph. Thrown by position player Brock Holt in 2022, it floated in so slowly that the batter didn't know whether to swing or laugh.

◎ The phrase "three strikes and you're out" originated from baseball but has since been adopted in legal systems, where some "three-strikes" laws impose harsher penalties on repeat offenders.

◎ The first baseball gloves were fingerless and looked more like padded hand protectors than modern gloves. Early players saw using a glove as a sign of weakness, and some refused to wear them.

AMERICAN FOOTBALL

◎ The NFL once had a game with a final score of 2-0. The Chicago Bears beat the Green Bay Packers in 1932 when a single safety was the only scoring play of the game.

◎ The first-ever professional football game was played on November 12, 1892, in Pittsburgh, Pennsylvania. The Allegheny Athletic Association paid a player named William "Pudge" Heffelfinger $500 to play, making him the first documented pro football player.

◎ The NFL was founded in 1920 as the American Professional Football Association (APFA). It was renamed the National Football League in 1922.

◎ The longest field goal in NFL history is 66 yards, set by Justin Tucker of the Baltimore Ravens in 2021. The ball bounced off the crossbar before going through, making it one of the most dramatic kicks ever.

◎ The Super Bowl is the most-watched television event in the United States every year. The record for the highest viewership was set during Super Bowl LIX in 2025, when the Philadelphia Eagles faced the Kansas City Chiefs, drawing 127.7 million viewers across TV and streaming. Before that, Super Bowl XLIX in 2015 held the record with 114.4 million viewers.

◎ The original Super Bowl trophy was named the "World Championship Game Trophy," but in 1970, it was renamed the Vince Lombardi Trophy in honor of the legendary Green Bay Packers coach.

◎ The Pittsburgh Steelers and the New England Patriots are tied for the most Super Bowl wins, with six championships each.

◎ The heaviest player in NFL history was Aaron Gibson, who weighed 410 pounds. Despite his massive size, he was an offensive lineman known for surprising agility.

◎ A standard NFL football weighs about 14-15 ounces and is made of cowhide leather. It takes about 600 cows per season to supply enough footballs for all the games.

◎ The fastest recorded speed for an NFL player in a game was 23.24 mph, set by Miami Dolphins running back Raheem Mostert in 2020. That's nearly as fast as a racehorse at full gallop.

◎ In 1943, due to player shortages during World War II, the Philadelphia Eagles and the Pittsburgh Steelers merged into a single team for one season. They were called the "Steagles."

◎ The coldest game in NFL history was the 1967 "Ice Bowl" between the Packers and Cowboys. The temperature at kickoff was -13°F with a wind chill of -48°F, but the game was still played.

◎ The shortest NFL player ever was Jack "Soapy" Shapiro, who stood just 5 feet 1 inch tall. He played a single game in 1929 as a halfback.

◎ The longest NFL game ever played lasted 82 minutes and 40 seconds of game time. The 1971 AFC Divisional Playoff between the Dolphins and Chiefs ended in double overtime, with Miami winning on a field goal.

◎ The first televised football game was broadcast in 1939 between the Brooklyn Dodgers and the Philadelphia Eagles. Only about 500 TV sets were in existence at the time.

◎ The huddle was invented by a deaf quarterback, Paul Hubbard, in 1894. He used it so his teammates could read his hand signals without the opposing team seeing them.

◎ The NFL didn't use official game balls with the "Duke" branding until 1941. The name comes from Wellington "Duke" Mara, the son of the New York Giants' first owner.

◎ The biggest comeback in NFL history happened in 1993 when the Buffalo Bills erased a 32-point deficit to beat the Houston Oilers in overtime.

◎ In 2013, the Denver Broncos and Seattle Seahawks played a Super Bowl where the first play resulted in a safety. It was the fastest score in Super Bowl history—just 12 seconds into the game.

◎ The Detroit Lions and the Dallas Cowboys always play on Thanksgiving, a tradition that started in 1934 for the Lions and 1966 for the Cowboys.

◎ Tom Brady has more Super Bowl wins (7) than any single franchise in NFL history. His career spanned 23 seasons, making him one of the most successful quarterbacks ever.

◎ The NFL once banned end zone celebrations but brought them back in 2017 after players and fans protested. The best-known celebrations include the "Ickey Shuffle," the "Lambeau Leap," and the "Dirty Bird."

◎ The Chicago Bears hold the record for the most players elected to the Pro Football Hall of Fame. They have over 30 enshrined legends.

◎ The highest-scoring game in NFL history was a 1966 matchup between the Washington Commanders (then Redskins) and the New York Giants, which ended 72-41.

◎ The NFL's first-ever draft pick was Jay Berwanger in 1936. The Philadelphia Eagles selected him, but he never played in the league because they couldn't afford his salary demands.

◎ The "tuck rule" was one of the most controversial rules in NFL history. It played a key role in a 2002 playoff game when a Tom Brady fumble was overturned, helping the Patriots advance and eventually win their first Super Bowl.

◎ NFL players weren't required to wear helmets until 1943. Before that, many players wore leather caps, and some played completely bareheaded.

◎ The Oakland Raiders once drafted a player they thought was someone else. In 1974, they selected a running back named "Mike" who had the same last name as the player they actually wanted, leading to one of the biggest draft mix-ups in history.

◎ The Arizona Cardinals are the oldest continuously operating football team in the United States. They were founded in 1898 as the Chicago Cardinals before moving to St. Louis and later Arizona.

⦿ The ancient Olympic Games were so important in Greece that warring city-states declared temporary truces just to allow athletes and spectators to travel safely to Olympia. Breaking the truce was considered a serious offense and could result in exile.

⦿ The first recorded Olympic champion was a cook named Coroebus, who won the stadion race (a short sprint) in 776 BCE. His victory earned him nothing but an olive wreath and eternal glory.

⦿ In the original Olympic Games, athletes competed completely naked. The word "gymnasium" even comes from the Greek word *gymnos*, meaning "naked."

⦿ The Olympics once included live pigeon shooting as an event. In the 1900 Paris Games, competitors shot down an estimated 300 birds before the gruesome event was never held again.

⦿ The 1904 Olympic marathon in St. Louis was a chaotic disaster. One runner nearly died from drinking rat poison, another hitched a ride in a car for miles, and the "winner" was disqualified after being carried across the finish line by his trainers.

⦿ The Olympic rings symbolize the five inhabited continents coming together in friendly competition. At least one of the five colors—blue, yellow, black, green, and red—appears in every national flag in the world.

◎ In the 1936 Berlin Olympics, two Japanese pole vaulters tied for second place. Instead of competing in a tiebreaker, they cut their silver and bronze medals in half and fused them together, creating two hybrid medals.

◎ The shortest Olympic event is the 50-meter freestyle swimming race, lasting just over 20 seconds. The longest is the men's 50 km race walk, which can take over four hours to complete.

◎ The first Olympic drug scandal happened in 1904 when an American marathon runner, Thomas Hicks, was given strychnine (a form of rat poison) mixed with brandy as a stimulant. Somehow, he survived and still won gold.

◎ The 1912 Olympics had the youngest-ever gold medalist: a 10-year-old boy who competed in rowing for the Dutch team. His identity is unknown because official records only listed him as "H.J."

◎ The 1928 Amsterdam Olympics were the first Games to allow women to compete in track and field. Before that, women were considered too fragile for running events, though they had been allowed in other sports since 1900.

◎ Finland's legendary runner Paavo Nurmi won nine Olympic gold medals but was banned from competing in the 1932 Olympics for receiving money in excess of travel reimbursements, violating strict amateurism rules. Despite this, he was so revered that he carried the Olympic torch at the 1952 Helsinki Games, cementing his legacy.

◎ At the 1932 Los Angeles Olympics, a Japanese official accidentally fired the starting pistol before the marathoners were ready. The runners took off in confusion, and officials had to chase them down to restart the race.

◎ The 1948 London Olympics had no Olympic Village due to post-war rationing. Male athletes slept in army barracks, while female competitors were housed in college dorms.

◎ The 1956 Melbourne Olympics featured equestrian events… in Sweden. Strict Australian quarantine laws forced organizers to hold the horse competitions in Stockholm five months before the main Games.

◎ Ethiopia's Abebe Bikila won the 1960 Olympic marathon barefoot. He didn't plan to run without shoes, but the pair he was given didn't fit well, so he just went without. He won again in 1964—this time wearing shoes.

◎ In 1964, a 17-year-old named Ewa Kłobukowska won gold in the 4×100m relay but was later subjected to a gender verification test. She failed due to an extra chromosome, though she was biologically female.

◎ A Japanese gymnast named Shun Fujimoto won gold in 1976 despite competing with a broken knee. He landed a perfect dismount in the team competition but revealed later that the landing had worsened his injury severely.

◎ The 1980 Moscow Olympics featured an opening ceremony mishap when a group of pigeons, released as part of the spectacle, flew straight into the Olympic flame and perished.

◎ In the 1988 Seoul Olympics, Canadian sprinter Ben Johnson shattered the 100m world record—only to be stripped of his medal three days later for steroid use. His scandal rocked the sports world and led to stricter doping regulations.

◎ The 1992 Barcelona Olympics introduced the first official Olympic mascot, Cobi, a cubist-style dog. Before that, mascots were unofficial and often strange, like the 1968 Grenoble Games' fuzzy toy called "Schuss."

◎ The 2000 Sydney Olympics had a hilarious mishap when an underdog swimmer, Eric "the Eel" Moussambani from Equatorial Guinea, struggled to finish his 100m freestyle heat. He had only trained for a few months and barely knew how to swim—but still set a personal best.

◎ Michael Phelps holds the record for the most Olympic medals, with 28, including 23 golds. If Phelps were his own country, he would rank above 150 nations in total Olympic gold medals.

◎ The 2008 Beijing Olympics featured a stunning opening ceremony directed by Zhang Yimou, but one detail was faked: the fireworks seen on TV included CGI effects added for dramatic effect.

◎ Usain Bolt broke three world records in the 2008 Beijing Olympics while smiling and celebrating before even finishing the races. His relaxed dominance made him one of the most iconic Olympians in history.

◎ The 2012 London Olympics had an odd moment when Queen Elizabeth II "jumped" out of a helicopter with James Bond (played by Daniel Craig) in a pre-recorded skit for the opening ceremony. The stunt fooled many into thinking she actually skydived.

◎ The 2016 Rio Olympics featured the first-ever Refugee Olympic Team, made up of displaced athletes from war-torn countries. The team marched under the Olympic flag and was met with a standing ovation.

◎ The 2020 Tokyo Olympics (held in 2021 due to COVID-19) had no live spectators for the first time in history. Athletes competed in near-empty arenas, making it one of the strangest and quietest Olympics ever.

◎ The Olympic flame has been to space. In 1996, astronauts aboard the Space Shuttle Atlantis carried an Olympic torch as part of the relay, though it wasn't lit for safety reasons.

RECORD-BREAKING STRUCTURES

⊚ The Burj Khalifa skyscraper in Dubai is so tall that you can watch the sunset twice. At 2,717 feet, the world's tallest building is so high that people on the top floors see the sun set later than those on the ground. In fact, Muslim residents in the tower are required to break their fasts at different times during Ramadan depending on their floor.

⊚ The longest bridge in the world could stretch across the English Channel—twice. The Danyang–Kunshan Grand Bridge in China spans 102.4 miles, carrying high-speed trains over rivers, valleys, and rice fields. It's so long that it would take an average person nearly two days to walk its entire length.

⊚ The world's largest stadium can fit an entire town. Rungrado 1st of May Stadium in North Korea holds up to 114,000 people—more than the entire population of Green Bay, Wisconsin. Despite its size, it's mostly used for mass gymnastics performances rather than sports.

⊚ The Eiffel Tower grows in the summer. Because metal expands in heat, the iron structure can grow up to seven inches taller in warm weather and shrink back in winter. Gustave Eiffel never mentioned this feature, but it makes his tower a living, breathing monument.

⊚ The deepest hole ever drilled could fit Mount Everest inside. The Kola Superdeep Borehole in Russia extends more than 40,000 feet into

172

the Earth's crust—so deep that scientists detected water where they didn't expect to find any. The intense heat and pressure eventually made further drilling impossible.

◎ The world's largest hotel has over 10,000 rooms—but no guests. The Abraj Kudai in Saudi Arabia, designed to be the biggest hotel in the world, remains unfinished due to financial setbacks. When completed, it will have 12 towers, five helipads, and 70 restaurants.

◎ The Leaning Tower of Pisa isn't the world's most tilted building. The Capital Gate Tower in Abu Dhabi leans at an 18-degree angle—four times more than Pisa's famous landmark. Unlike the Tower of Pisa, however, its tilt was entirely intentional.

◎ The world's longest tunnel took 17 years to complete. The Gotthard Base Tunnel in Switzerland runs for 35.5 miles under the Alps, allowing trains to pass through the mountains instead of climbing over them. The tunnel is so deep that it takes nearly 20 minutes to travel through at full speed.

◎ A skyscraper in China was built in just 19 days. The Mini Sky City in Changsha, a 57-story building, was constructed using modular sections that workers assembled at a breakneck speed. It's earthquake-resistant and eco-friendly, proving that speed doesn't always mean cutting corners.

◎ The world's largest pyramid isn't in Egypt. The Great Pyramid of Cholula in Mexico is the biggest by volume, covering a larger area than the Great Pyramid of Giza. It's so massive that early explorers mistook it for a hill.

◎ The tallest statue in the world is almost twice the height of the Statue of Liberty. India's Statue of Unity stands at 597 feet, towering over all other statues on the planet. It was built to honor Sardar Patel, one of India's founding fathers.

◎ The longest escalator in the world isn't in a mall—it's a transit system. The Central–Mid-Levels Escalator in Hong Kong stretches over 2,600 feet and moves commuters through the city's steep streets. It even has stopping points for restaurants and shops along the way.

◎ The largest palace in the world is still in use. The Forbidden City in Beijing, with over 980 buildings, is the world's largest palace complex. Despite its historical status, parts of it are still used by the Chinese government.

◎ The world's largest indoor waterfall is inside an airport. Singapore's Jewel Changi Airport features a 130-foot-tall waterfall cascading through the center of a lush, tropical garden. It turns a layover into a sightseeing adventure.

◎ The fastest elevator in the world moves at 46 miles per hour. Inside the Shanghai Tower, this high-speed lift takes passengers from the ground to the 119th floor in just 55 seconds. It's so smooth that most people barely feel the acceleration.

◎ The world's largest swimming pool is over half a mile long. Located in Chile, the San Alfonso del Mar pool holds 66 million gallons of water and is so vast that it's navigable by kayak. It's more like a man-made lagoon than a traditional pool.

◎ The tallest roller coaster on Earth is terrifyingly high. Kingda Ka, located in New Jersey, reaches a height of 456 feet and launches riders from 0 to 128 mph in just 3.5 seconds. If you're afraid of heights, this one isn't for you.

◎ The largest cave in the world has its own weather system. Hang Sơn Đoòng in Vietnam is so massive that it contains jungles, rivers, and even clouds inside its chambers. Some of its passages could fit an entire New York City block.

◎ The longest staircase in the world has 11,674 steps. The Niesenbahn funicular railway in Switzerland has a maintenance staircase that zigzags up the mountainside for over two miles. It's open to the public once a year for an extreme endurance race.

◎ The world's largest sundial is big enough to walk through. The Samrat Yantra in India is a 90-foot-high sundial built in the 18th century. It can tell the time down to two-second accuracy—no batteries required.

◎ The longest-running construction project in history is still ongoing. The Sagrada Familia in Barcelona has been under construction since 1882 and is still unfinished. Architects estimate it may finally be completed by 2026—144 years after it began.

◎ A hotel made entirely of ice is rebuilt every year. Sweden's Icehotel is carved from frozen blocks each winter, only to melt away in spring. Every year, new artists create fresh designs, ensuring no two visits are the same.

◎ The largest cruise ship in the world is like a floating city. Royal Caribbean's *Icon of the Seas* is so massive that it has its own neighborhoods, a park, and a waterpark with the tallest slide at sea. It can carry more than 7,500 passengers.

◎ The world's longest zipline is over a mile and a half long. Located in the UAE, the Jebel Jais Flight zipline sends thrill-seekers soaring at speeds up to 93 mph over mountain peaks. It's so long that riders need a parachute-like braking system to slow down at the end.

◎ The tallest hotel in the world is in Dubai. The Gevora Hotel stands at 1,168 feet, towering over every other hotel on Earth. Its rooftop pool offers a dizzying view of the skyline.

◎ The oldest wooden building in the world has survived for over 1,300 years. Japan's Horyu-ji Temple was built in 607 AD and has withstood earthquakes, fires, and wars. Its secret? A unique wooden joinery technique that absorbs shocks without nails.

◎ A single skyscraper in Tokyo generates its own power. The Mode Gakuen Cocoon Tower has a wind power system built into its design, helping supply its own electricity. It's a rare example of a self-sustaining high-rise.

CRAZY CAT FACTS

⊚ A cat's purr vibrates at a frequency between 25 and 150 hertz—amazingly, the same range that promotes healing in bones and tissues. Some scientists believe cats might instinctively purr to help themselves recover from injuries.

⊚ Unlike most animals, cats don't have a sweet tooth. Their taste buds lack the receptor for sweetness, meaning they'll never crave sugary treats like humans do.

⊚ The world's oldest known pet cat was found buried alongside its owner in a 9,500-year-old grave in Cyprus. This suggests humans and cats were companions long before ancient Egypt made them famous.

⊚ Morris the Cat, the finicky feline from 9Lives commercials, was originally a shelter rescue. The first Morris, discovered in 1968 at a Chicago animal shelter, became a TV sensation known for his snarky attitude and refusal to eat anything but 9Lives cat food. His popularity led to a book deal and a brief stint in politics when fans joked about his presidential campaign.

⊚ The first cat in space was a French feline named Félicette, launched in 1963. Electrodes implanted in her brain transmitted neural signals back to Earth, proving cats could survive space travel—though she was not as lucky upon returning.

◎ The first animated TV cat, Felix, debuted in silent films before becoming a television icon. Created in 1919, Felix the Cat became so famous that he was the first image ever broadcast on American television in 1928 as part of an RCA test signal. His magic bag of tricks and mischievous grin kept him popular for decades.

◎ A cat's whiskers aren't just for decoration—they're highly sensitive touch sensors that help cats navigate tight spaces, detect air currents, and even judge distances when hunting. If a cat's whiskers touch the sides of a space, it knows whether it can fit through.

◎ In the Middle Ages, Pope Gregory IX declared that cats were associated with witchcraft, leading to mass killings of felines. Ironically, the loss of cats contributed to an explosion in the rat population, worsening the spread of the Black Death.

◎ A cat's meow is actually a language designed for humans. While kittens meow at their mothers, adult cats almost never meow at each other—only at people to get their attention.

◎ The world's longest cat, Stewie, measured an astonishing 48.5 inches from nose to tail. That's longer than some small dogs!

◎ Orangey, the tabby who played Cat in *Breakfast at Tiffany's*, was a true Hollywood diva. He was trained to sit still on cue but was known for running off set and being difficult to work with. Despite his antics, he won two Patsy Awards (the animal equivalent of an Oscar), making him one of the most decorated feline actors in history.

◎ Cats can rotate their ears a full 180 degrees and move them independently. This allows them to pinpoint sounds with incredible accuracy, even while their body remains completely still.

◎ In 2013, a cat named Oscar became famous for predicting death. Living in a Rhode Island nursing home, he would curl up next to terminally ill patients just before they passed away—his accuracy was eerily high.

◎ The world's wealthiest cat, Blackie, inherited $12.5 million when his owner left him a fortune in his will. Meanwhile, the man's relatives received nothing.

◎ Ever wondered why cats knock things off tables? This behavior mimics how they hunt—poking and prodding prey to test its movement before striking. Plus, they love watching humans react.

◎ A group of cats is called a "clowder," while a group of kittens is known as a "kindle." Meanwhile, a lone, unowned cat is often referred to as a "feral" or "stray," depending on its level of socialization.

◎ Unlike humans, cats walk by moving both right legs together, then both left legs. Only camels and giraffes share this same unusual walking pattern.

◎ Cats can drink seawater to survive! Their kidneys are so efficient at filtering out salt that they can rehydrate from ocean water—something most mammals, including humans, can't do.

◎ The Guinness World Record for the loudest purr belongs to a cat named Merlin, whose purr reached 67.8 decibels. That's as loud as a vacuum cleaner!

◎ In Japan, a cat named Tama was appointed as a train station master and given a tiny uniform. Her presence boosted tourism so much that she was promoted to "Super Station Master."

◎ Cats have a unique "righting reflex" that allows them to almost always land on their feet when falling. This ability kicks in as early as three weeks old, giving them an uncanny sense of balance.

◎ A cat's nose print is as unique as a human fingerprint. No two cats have the same pattern of ridges and bumps, making it a potential (though wildly impractical) method for feline identification.

◎ The average house cat can run up to 30 mph—faster than Usain Bolt at his peak. Good luck catching one when it decides it doesn't want to go to the vet.

⊚ Ancient Egyptians loved their cats so much that families would shave their eyebrows in mourning if their pet died. Killing a cat, even accidentally, was punishable by death.

⊚ The oldest recorded pet cat, Crème Puff, lived to an astonishing 38 years old—more than double the typical feline lifespan. She was raised on a bizarre diet that included bacon and eggs.

⊚ There's a breed of cat called the "Lykoi," also known as the "werewolf cat." These cats have a patchy coat and a haunting stare, making them look like tiny werewolves.

⊚ The world's first cat video dates back to 1894. It was filmed by Thomas Edison's team and featured two cats boxing in a miniature ring.

⊚ The ancient Norse goddess Freyja rode in a chariot pulled by giant cats. Because of this, farmers believed feeding stray cats would bring them good harvests.

⊚ A cat's pupils can change size dramatically, not just in response to light but also due to emotions. Dilated pupils can indicate excitement, fear, or even aggression.

⊚ The first known cat to circumnavigate the globe was a feline named Trim, who sailed with explorer Matthew Flinders in the early 1800s. He was so beloved that statues of him now stand in multiple countries.

⊚ Some cats are naturally polydactyl, meaning they have extra toes. One cat named Jake holds the record with 28 toes—almost double the usual amount!

⊚ The immortal jellyfish can live forever—sort of. *Turritopsis dohrnii* has the ability to revert its cells back to a juvenile state, essentially restarting its life cycle. In theory, it could do this indefinitely, making it biologically immortal—unless it gets eaten.

⊚ Octopuses have three hearts. Two pump blood to the gills, while the third sends it to the rest of the body. When an octopus swims, the main heart actually stops beating, which is why they prefer crawling over swimming.

⊚ The mantis shrimp punches with such force that it can crack aquarium glass and shatter crab shells. Its lightning-fast strike reaches speeds of 50 mph—so fast it momentarily creates temperatures nearly as hot as the sun.

⊚ Elephants can "hear" with their feet. They detect seismic vibrations from miles away by using the sensitive cells in their footpads. This helps them sense approaching danger—like a predator or an oncoming storm—before it arrives.

⊚ Some frogs can survive being frozen solid. The wood frog endures Arctic winters by freezing nearly 70% of its body water. Its heart stops, its blood thickens, and yet, when spring arrives, it thaws and hops away like nothing happened.

◎ The world's smallest mammal is lighter than a penny. The bumblebee bat weighs about 2 grams and is small enough to fit on the tip of your finger. Despite its tiny size, it's a skilled hunter, catching insects mid-flight.

◎ Crows can recognize human faces. They remember people who treat them well—and those who don't. Some have even been observed "gossiping" about untrustworthy humans and teaching their young to avoid them.

◎ A species of fish produces blue blood. The ocellated icefish, found in Antarctica, has antifreeze proteins in its blood to survive freezing waters. It's the only vertebrate known to lack hemoglobin, giving its blood a ghostly, transparent blue tint.

◎ The pistol shrimp stuns prey with sound. It snaps its claw shut so fast that it creates a bubble traveling at 60 mph, producing a noise louder than a gunshot. The resulting shockwave is enough to knock out small fish instantly.

◎ The world's longest migration belongs to a bird. The Arctic tern flies from the Arctic to the Antarctic and back every year, covering over 4,000 miles. In its lifetime, it travels the equivalent of three round trips to the moon.

◎ Sloths can hold their breath longer than dolphins. By slowing their heart rate, sloths can hold their breath for up to 40 minutes underwater. This helps them avoid predators like jaguars when they take a swim.

◎ A chameleon's tongue is longer than its body. It can shoot out in just 0.07 seconds to snatch prey. The sticky tip acts like a high-speed suction cup, ensuring that lunch doesn't escape.

◎ A single colony of army ants can have millions of members. These relentless hunters move together in waves, devouring almost anything in their path. Some swarms have been known to take down small mammals.

◎ The snapping shrimp generates one of the loudest sounds in the ocean. By snapping its claw shut at incredible speed, it creates a shockwave that momentarily reaches 210 decibels—powerful enough to stun or kill small fish.

◎ A sea cucumber can eject its organs as a defense mechanism. When threatened, it shoots out its intestines and other internal organs to confuse predators. Incredibly, it regrows them within weeks.

◎ The fastest land animal isn't the cheetah—it's a mite. The Paratarsotomus macropalpis, a tiny mite, can run at speeds equivalent to 322 body lengths per second. If a human could do that, they'd be running at over 1,300 mph.

◎ Some turtles breathe through their butts. Species like the Fitzroy River turtle absorb oxygen through specialized sacs near their tail, allowing them to stay underwater for extended periods. Scientists call this cloacal respiration, but "butt breathing" is more fun.

◎ A jellyfish's sting can remain active long after it dies. Even detached tentacles can still sting unsuspecting swimmers. Some species, like the box jellyfish, have venom strong enough to stop a human heart.

◎ A kangaroo can't walk backward. Due to the structure of its muscular tail and powerful legs, hopping forward is its only option. This is why the kangaroo appears on Australia's coat of arms—it symbolizes progress.

◎ The axolotl can regenerate its limbs, heart, and even parts of its brain. Unlike most animals, this salamander doesn't scar when injured. Scientists are studying it in hopes of unlocking regenerative medicine for humans.

◎ A blue whale's heart weighs as much as a small car and beats so powerfully that it can be detected from miles away using specialized equipment. When it dives, its heart rate slows to just two beats per minute to conserve oxygen.

◎ Penguins propose with pebbles. Male Adélie and Gentoo penguins search for the smoothest, most perfect pebble to present to a female. If she accepts it, they become lifelong mates.

◎ A flea can jump 200 times its body length. If humans had the same ability, we'd be able to leap over skyscrapers. This insane jumping power is due to a spring-like protein in their legs called resilin.

◎ A mother octopus sacrifices herself for her eggs. After laying thousands of eggs, a female octopus stops eating and devotes herself to guarding them. She dies shortly after they hatch, making one of the most extreme maternal sacrifices in the animal kingdom.

◎ The coconut crab is the largest land-dwelling arthropod. Weighing up to nine pounds with a leg span over three feet, it can crack open coconuts with its powerful claws. It has also been known to steal shiny objects from campsites.

◎ The only known "venomous" primate is the slow loris. It secretes a toxin from its elbow that, when mixed with saliva, creates a venomous bite. This unique defense makes it one of the rarest venomous mammals.

◎ The glass frog has nearly transparent skin. If you look at its belly, you can see its internal organs, including its beating heart. Scientists believe this camouflage helps it blend in with the leaves it rests on.

◎ Spiders can fly using electricity. Some spiders use a technique called "ballooning," releasing silk threads that catch electric fields in the atmosphere, lifting them into the air. Some have even been found miles above the Earth's surface.

FACTS ABOUT DOGS

◎ The Basenji is known as the "barkless dog" because it doesn't bark like other breeds. Instead, it makes a unique yodeling sound called a "barroo," which comes from its unusually shaped larynx.

◎ Dogs have a sense of time and can tell the difference between one hour and five hours. Studies show they anticipate daily routines, which is why they often wait by the door when it's time for their owner to return.

◎ The world's oldest known dog lived to be 31 years old. Bobi, a Rafeiro do Alentejo from Portugal, held the Guinness World Record before passing away in 2023.

◎ A Greyhound could beat a cheetah in a long-distance race. While cheetahs are faster in short bursts, Greyhounds can maintain a speed of 35 mph for several miles, while a cheetah tires out after 30 seconds.

◎ A dog's nose print is as unique as a human fingerprint. Some companies even use nose prints for pet identification.

◎ The ancient Chinese Emperors kept Pekingese dogs in their robes as living hand warmers. These tiny, lion-like dogs were so sacred that only royalty could own them.

⊚ A Labrador Retriever once served as the mayor of a small town in California. Bosco, a black Lab, won an election against two human candidates and served as "mayor" of Sunol for over a decade.

⊚ Some stray dogs in Moscow have learned to navigate the subway system. They hop on and off trains at specific stops to find food and return to their sleeping areas.

⊚ The Norwegian Lundehund is one of the rarest breeds and has six toes on each foot. This unique trait helped them climb rocky cliffs to hunt puffins, which were once a food source in Norway.

⊚ The world's heaviest dog breed is the English Mastiff. The largest recorded Mastiff, named Zorba, weighed 343 pounds and was over 8 feet long from nose to tail.

⊚ Dalmatian puppies are born completely white. Their signature black spots don't appear until they are about two weeks old.

⊚ The Beatles' song *A Day in the Life* contains a frequency only dogs can hear. Paul McCartney admitted adding the high-pitched sound as a secret treat for canine listeners.

⊚ Some dogs have such strong scent detection abilities that they can sniff out diseases like cancer, diabetes, and even malaria. Medical detection dogs are trained to identify specific odors linked to illnesses.

⊚ The phrase "raining cats and dogs" may have originated from old European cities where heavy rain would wash dead animals from rooftops and streets. Another theory links it to Norse mythology and storm gods associated with dogs and wolves.

⊚ A dog's tail wag direction can reveal its emotions. Studies show that wagging more to the right indicates happiness, while wagging more to the left suggests anxiety or stress.

⊚ Siberian Huskies have built-in snowshoes. Their furry paws have a thick layer of fur between the toes, helping them walk on ice and snow without slipping.

◎ In 1925, a Siberian Husky named Balto led a sled dog team on the final leg of a 674-mile journey to deliver life-saving medicine to Nome, Alaska. His statue stands in New York's Central Park to honor his heroic feat.

◎ Dogs can learn up to 250 words and gestures. The most intelligent breeds, like Border Collies and Poodles, have the language comprehension of a 2-year-old child.

◎ The Great Pyrenees was bred to guard livestock in the mountains, and its thick double coat protects it from freezing temperatures. Some modern Great Pyrenees still work as flock guardians today.

◎ A dog named Hachiko waited at a train station in Japan every day for nearly 10 years after his owner passed away. His loyalty became legendary, and a statue was erected in his honor outside Tokyo's Shibuya Station.

◎ Basset Hounds have the longest ears of any breed. Their long ears help sweep scents toward their powerful noses, making them excellent trackers.

◎ The Chihuahua is the smallest dog breed, but it has the biggest brain relative to its body size. Despite their tiny stature, they are known for their sharp intelligence and bold personalities.

◎ The Saluki is one of the oldest dog breeds, dating back over 4,000 years. Ancient Egyptian pharaohs kept them as prized hunting dogs, and they were even mummified alongside their owners.

◎ Newfoundlands are natural lifeguards and have webbed feet to help them swim. They have been known to save drowning people by pulling them to shore.

◎ Dogs have three eyelids. The third eyelid, called the nictitating membrane, helps protect and lubricate their eyes, especially in breeds that are prone to dry eye or irritation.

◎ The Bloodhound's sense of smell is so strong that its tracking evidence is admissible in court. A Bloodhound's nose has around 300 million scent receptors, making it one of the best tracking dogs in the world.

◎ The Shiba Inu breed has a unique "Shiba scream"—a high-pitched, dramatic yelp they make when excited or unhappy. Some Shibas let out an ear-piercing scream just from getting their nails trimmed.

◎ Dogs curl up when they sleep as an instinct to protect their vital organs. This behavior dates back to their wild ancestors, who slept curled up to conserve heat and stay hidden from predators.

◎ The world's tallest dog was a Great Dane named Zeus, who stood at an astonishing 44 inches tall at the shoulder. Standing on his hind legs, he was over 7 feet tall—taller than most humans.

FUN FOOD FACTS

⦿ Honey never spoils. Archaeologists have found pots of honey in ancient Egyptian tombs that are over 3,000 years old—and still perfectly edible. Its long shelf life is due to low moisture content and natural antibacterial properties.

⦿ The world's most expensive coffee is made from poop. Kopi Luwak coffee beans are eaten and partially digested by civet cats before being collected from their droppings. The fermentation process inside the animal gives the coffee its unique flavor and an eye-watering price tag.

⦿ Strawberries aren't really berries, but bananas are. Botanically speaking, a berry has seeds and pulp that develop from a single flower ovary—making bananas, cucumbers, and eggplants true berries. Strawberries don't qualify because their seeds are on the outside.

⦿ Cucumbers are also technically fruits. Since they develop from a flower and contain seeds, cucumbers fall under the botanical definition of fruit. So yes, your salad is sneakily full of fruit.

⦿ A pineapple takes years to grow—far longer than most fruits. From planting to harvest, it can take up to two years to fully mature, and each plant produces only one pineapple at a time.

◎ Peppers don't actually burn your mouth—they trick your brain. The compound capsaicin binds to pain receptors that usually detect heat, making your body think you're on fire. Drinking water only spreads the burn, but dairy products can help neutralize it.

◎ Apples float because they're 25% air. This built-in buoyancy is why bobbing for apples works—they naturally rise to the surface of water. It's also why apples are so satisfyingly crisp when you bite into them.

◎ There's a fruit that tastes like chocolate pudding. The black sapote, sometimes called the "chocolate pudding fruit," has a rich, dark flesh with a sweet, cocoa-like flavor. It's a dream come true for chocolate lovers trying to eat healthy.

◎ McDonald's once made bubblegum-flavored broccoli. It was an attempt to make vegetables more appealing to kids, but it failed spectacularly. Children found the taste confusing, and the idea was quickly scrapped.

◎ Cheese is basically milk that's been "rotted" on purpose. The cheese-making process involves controlled decomposition through bacteria and enzymes, transforming fresh milk into solid, flavorful curds. Some cheeses, like Casu Marzu, even contain live maggots to enhance fermentation.

◎ Carrots weren't always orange. Originally, carrots were purple, yellow, or white. The familiar orange variety was selectively bred by Dutch farmers in the 17th century as a tribute to the ruling House of Orange.

◎ One of the rarest cheeses in the world is made from donkey milk. Pule cheese, produced in Serbia, requires over 25 liters of donkey milk to make just one kilogram. It sells for thousands of dollars per pound due to its labor-intensive production.

◎ The holes in Swiss cheese are made by bacteria burps. A bacterium called *Propionibacterium* produces carbon dioxide during fermentation, forming the characteristic holes, or "eyes." Cheesemakers can adjust the size of the holes by controlling the bacteria's diet.

◎ Peanuts aren't nuts. They're legumes, meaning they belong to the same family as beans and lentils. True nuts, like almonds and walnuts, grow on trees, while peanuts grow underground.

◎ Worcestershire sauce is made with fermented anchovies. The popular condiment gets its umami-rich flavor from anchovies that are left to ferment in barrels for up to 18 months. Despite its fishy origins, it's often used in beef dishes and even Bloody Mary cocktails.

◎ Cotton candy was invented by a dentist. In 1897, dentist William Morrison co-invented the first cotton candy machine, originally calling it "fairy floss." He clearly had mixed feelings about dental health.

◎ Gummy bears were inspired by dancing bears. In the 1920s, German candy maker Hans Riegel created the first gummy bear, inspired by the trained bear acts seen at fairs. His company, Haribo, still dominates the gummy candy industry today.

◎ The world's oldest known recipe is for beer. A 4,000-year-old Sumerian tablet contains a detailed method for brewing a type of barley beer. Ancient civilizations considered beer a staple food rather than just a beverage.

◎ Cashews grow on the outside of fruit. The cashew "nut" is actually the seed of the cashew apple, hanging from the bottom of the fruit like a little hook. The shell contains toxic oils, which is why cashews are never sold in their raw, natural state.

◎ Ice cream was once considered a health food. In the 18th century, doctors believed ice cream could cure diseases and recommended it as a cooling treatment. Unfortunately, this belief didn't hold up, but it did make for some happy patients.

◎ Potatoes were once banned in France from 1748 to 1772. Some feared they caused disease, while others simply saw them as food for livestock. A pharmacist named Antoine-Augustin Parmentier later convinced the public of their value by hosting potato feasts for aristocrats.

⊚ The world's spiciest chili pepper is so hot, it can cause hallucinations. The Carolina Reaper averages 1.6 million Scoville heat units, with some reaching over 2.2 million. Eating one raw can lead to intense pain, dizziness, and even a temporary sense of euphoria.

⊚ Pineapple works as a meat tenderizer. It contains bromelain, an enzyme that breaks down protein, which is why it can make your tongue feel tingly when you eat too much. This also means pineapple juice can turn tough cuts of meat into tender perfection.

⊚ Saffron is more expensive than gold. Harvested from the delicate stigma of the crocus flower, saffron requires thousands of flowers to produce just a few grams. Its high price is due to the labor-intensive process and its rich, aromatic flavor.

⊚ The chocolate bar was originally a drink. The ancient Maya and Aztecs consumed chocolate as a bitter, spiced beverage mixed with chili peppers and water. Sugar was only added centuries later, transforming chocolate into the sweet treat we know today.

⊚ Garlic can be used as glue. Its sticky juice acts as a natural adhesive strong enough to bond glass together. Medieval monks reportedly used garlic to repair cracked windows in monasteries.

⊚ There's a soup that has been cooking for over 50 years. In Bangkok, a restaurant has kept a pot of soup simmering continuously since the 1970s, adding new ingredients daily. This technique, known as "perpetual stew," creates a flavor profile that deepens over decades.

CURIOUS CUSTOMS

◉ In Spain, La Tomatina is the world's largest food fight, where thousands gather in Buñol to throw overripe tomatoes at each other. The origins of this messy tradition are unclear, but it's been an annual event since the 1940s.

◉ In Thailand, it's considered rude to point your feet at someone, as feet are seen as the lowest and dirtiest part of the body. Conversely, touching someone's head, the most sacred part, is also taboo.

◉ In Japan, slurping noodles loudly is not bad manners—it's a sign you're enjoying your meal. It's also believed to enhance the flavor by aerating the broth.

◉ South Koreans celebrate a second Valentine's Day called Black Day. On April 14, single people gather to eat black bean noodles (jjajangmyeon) and commiserate over their lack of romance.

◉ In Denmark, if you're unmarried by the time you turn 25, friends may cover you in cinnamon. If you're still single at 30, they upgrade to pepper. This tradition dates back centuries and was originally aimed at traveling spice merchants who remained bachelors.

◉ In Germany, people celebrate a person's 50th birthday with a "golden wedding" ceremony—even if they're not married. Friends and family decorate their home with golden ornaments and flowers as a way to honor their life achievements.

◎ In the Philippines, a Christmas celebration isn't complete without a giant lantern festival. The city of San Fernando is famous for creating dazzling, intricate star-shaped lanterns, some as large as houses, made from thousands of lights.

◎ In Mongolia, guests are often welcomed with a bowl of fermented mare's milk called airag. Refusing it is considered impolite, so visitors have to develop a taste for its tangy, slightly alcoholic flavor.

◎ In China, people eat long noodles on their birthday, symbolizing a wish for a long life. Cutting or biting the noodles before swallowing is believed to bring bad luck.

◎ In Greece, spitting is considered a way to ward off bad luck. While no one actually spits saliva, a symbolic "ftou ftou ftou" is often said after hearing bad news or giving a compliment to prevent misfortune.

◎ In Scotland, before a wedding, some brides and grooms are subjected to the "blackening" ritual. Friends and family douse them in rotten food, molasses, feathers, or flour and parade them through the streets—it's all meant to bring good luck in marriage.

◎ In Brazil, the "Festa de São João" (Festival of St. John) is a midsummer celebration where people dress as country folk, light bonfires, and even fake marriages for fun. It's a lively and colorful tradition dating back to Portuguese settlers.

◎ In India, some widows break bangles and wipe away their sindoor (red hair powder) as a sign of mourning. However, in recent years, movements have encouraged widows to celebrate life rather than withdrawing from festivities.

◎ In Mexico, the "Day of the Dead" (Día de los Muertos) isn't a sad occasion—it's a festive time to celebrate deceased loved ones. Families create altars with food, candles, and marigolds, believing the spirits return to enjoy their favorite meals.

◎ In Finland, there's a national Wife-Carrying Championship. Competitors race through an obstacle course carrying their wives (or any female partner) on their backs. The prize? The woman's weight in beer.

◎ In Sweden, it's common to pause for "fika," a daily coffee break with pastries, emphasizing relaxation and socialization. It's not just about caffeine—it's a cultural institution of slowing down and enjoying the moment.

◎ In Italy, on New Year's Eve, some people throw old furniture and belongings out the window. The tradition symbolizes getting rid of the past to make space for good fortune in the coming year.

◎ In Japan, there's a festival where sumo wrestlers try to make babies cry. The belief is that a loud, strong cry will bring the baby good health and drive away evil spirits.

◎ In Bolivia, on All Saints' Day, families bring human skulls, known as "ñatitas," to cemeteries and decorate them with flowers and cigarettes. It's believed these skulls bring protection and guidance to their owners.

◎ In Portugal, there's a tradition called "Bananeiro," where people gather on Christmas Eve at a banana warehouse to drink beer and celebrate with friends before heading to family dinners. It's an unofficial but beloved holiday custom.

◎ In Turkey, on New Year's Eve, people smash pomegranates on their doorstep. The number of seeds that scatter represents the amount of good fortune the household will receive in the coming year.

◎ In Russia, some people write down their New Year's wishes on a piece of paper, burn it, and mix the ashes into a glass of champagne— then drink it to make their wish come true.

◎ In Hungary, it's considered bad luck to clink beer glasses when making a toast. This stems from a historical event in 1848, when Austrian soldiers celebrated Hungary's defeat by clinking their beer mugs together.

◎ In Ethiopia, the New Year (Enkutatash) is celebrated in September with fresh yellow flowers covering the fields. The name means "gift of jewels," referencing the legend of the Queen of Sheba returning from her visit to King Solomon.

◎ In Taiwan, the Ghost Festival is dedicated to honoring wandering spirits. Offerings of food and money are left outside to appease the ghosts and prevent bad luck. It's considered unlucky to whistle at night, as it might attract restless spirits.

◎ In New Zealand, the Māori welcome the new year with Matariki, a festival tied to the Pleiades star cluster. It's a time for storytelling, remembering ancestors, and celebrating the harvest with feasts.

◎ In Vietnam, people release carp fish into rivers before the Lunar New Year. The belief is that these fish carry the Kitchen Gods to heaven to report on the household's affairs for the past year.

◎ In Switzerland, people intentionally drop ice cream on the ground as part of their New Year's traditions. It's believed that sacrificing something sweet will bring abundance and good fortune.

◎ In the Czech Republic, fortune-telling is a key part of Christmas Eve traditions. One method involves slicing an apple in half—if the seeds form a star, good luck is coming, but if they form a cross, misfortune may be ahead.

◎ There's a place in the U.S. where no laws technically exist. A loophole in Yellowstone National Park, known as the "Zone of Death," theoretically allows someone to commit a crime and escape punishment due to a jurisdictional oversight. No one has tested it—yet.

◎ The U.S. government still owns a giant cheese. In 1835, President Andrew Jackson received a 1,400-pound wheel of cheddar. It was left sitting in the White House for two years before he gave it away. The stench reportedly lingered for months.

◎ The Library of Congress archives every single tweet ever posted. That means your embarrassing 2009 Twitter phase is now a permanent part of U.S. history.

◎ A single vote once saved a U.S. president from removal. In 1868, President Andrew Johnson faced impeachment, and the Senate vote came down to one deciding ballot. He was acquitted by just one vote, narrowly avoiding removal from office in one of the closest impeachment trials in American history.

◎ The town of Monowi, Nebraska, has a population of one. The sole resident, Elsie Eiler, is the mayor, librarian, and bartender of her self-run community. She even grants herself a liquor license each year.

◎ The Pentagon has twice as many bathrooms as necessary. When it was built in the 1940s, segregation laws required separate restrooms for Black and white employees. The extra bathrooms remain today, unused but still part of the structure.

◎ There's a town in Pennsylvania called Intercourse. It's not alone in the state—other nearby towns include Blue Ball and Bird-in-Hand. Yes, all are on the map, and yes, they get a lot of stolen road signs.

◎ There's an underground city beneath the streets of Seattle. After the Great Seattle Fire of 1889, the city was rebuilt on top of the ruins, leaving an entire network of abandoned streets and storefronts below the surface.

◎ You can walk from Russia to Alaska—sort of. In winter, the Bering Strait sometimes freezes between the Diomede Islands, making it possible to trek between the two countries. Just don't expect border patrol to be thrilled about it.

◎ The shortest war in U.S. history lasted just a few minutes. In 1838, a dispute between Maine and Canada led to the Aroostook War, which ended without a single casualty after both sides realized they didn't actually want to fight.

◎ There's an island in Maine that belongs to Canada—but it's in U.S. waters. Machias Seal Island is claimed by both nations, leading to an ongoing dispute. To this day, both American and Canadian lighthouse keepers live there to maintain their country's presence.

◎ A town in Minnesota once elected a dog as its mayor. Duke the Great Pyrenees served as the ceremonial leader of Cormorant, MN, winning multiple terms before retiring. His approval ratings were probably higher than most politicians'.

◎ There's an official UFO welcome center in South Carolina. Built in 1994 by Jody Pendarvis, this homemade alien landing pad in Bowman, SC, is ready for extraterrestrial visitors—if they ever decide to stop by.

The Empire State Building has its own ZIP code. With over 100 floors and thousands of workers, it was assigned 10118 to handle all its incoming mail.

A town in Pennsylvania has been on fire for over 60 years. The underground coal fire in Centralia, PA has been burning since 1962, creating an eerie ghost town above ground.

The U.S. once had a camel cavalry. In the 1850s, the Army imported camels for desert transport in the Southwest. They worked well, but the Civil War ended the experiment, and the camels were set loose or sold.

Every state has its own official state drink. Most pick milk, but Rhode Island has coffee milk, while Nebraska proudly claims Kool-Aid as its signature beverage.

There's a lake in Oregon with a floating tree stump that has been bobbing upright for over 100 years. Called the "Old Man of the Lake," it drifts unpredictably around Crater Lake, sometimes covering great distances in a single day.

The Liberty Bell has been to all 50 states—sort of. In 1950, the U.S. government commissioned 55 exact replicas of the Liberty Bell, sending them to every state and U.S. territory to promote patriotism.

The U.S. Supreme Court once ruled that tomatoes are vegetables—even though they're technically fruit. The decision came in an 1893 case about tariffs on imported produce. Legally speaking, tomatoes are veggies in America.

There's a 1,000-year-old tree in California with a drive-through tunnel carved into its trunk. The Chandelier Tree in Leggett, CA, is a living redwood that somehow survived having a hole cut through it for cars to pass.

The Statue of Liberty was originally meant to be a lighthouse. It was equipped with a massive torch, but the light wasn't bright enough to be useful for ships. It officially served as a lighthouse from 1886 to 1902 before being retired.

◎ George Washington was so good at distilling whiskey that he became one of the largest whiskey producers in the country after his presidency. His Mount Vernon distillery is still operational today.

◎ There's an abandoned subway station under New York City that looks straight out of a movie. The old City Hall station, with its elegant tiled arches and chandeliers, has been closed since 1945 but is still visible if you take a certain subway loop.

TIME TRAVEL

⊚ Time travel is technically possible—but only forward. According to Einstein's theory of relativity, the faster you move through space, the slower you experience time. Astronauts on the International Space Station age slightly slower than people on Earth, making them real-life time travelers.

⊚ In 2000, a man named John Titor appeared in online forums claiming to be a time traveler from 2036. He described future events and even posted schematics for a supposed time machine. His predictions never came true, but his legend still lingers in internet folklore.

⊚ In 1980, a group of Spanish soldiers reported driving into a mysterious fog near Seville—only to find themselves suddenly in the 16th century. They claimed they saw people in medieval clothing and an ancient fortress before the fog lifted and returned them to modern times.

⊚ Black holes could, in theory, allow for time travel. If you could survive falling into a rotating black hole, you might enter a closed time loop, where time bends back on itself. The only problem? No one knows if you'd ever escape.

⊚ The "Grandfather Paradox" is one of time travel's biggest problems. If you traveled back in time and prevented your grandfather from meeting your grandmother, you would never be born—so how could you have traveled back in the first place?

◎ The planet Mercury might hold the key to understanding time loops. Due to its strange orbit and proximity to the Sun, there are points where a day lasts longer than a year, making it a natural case study for warped time perception.

◎ Some physicists believe time is an illusion. According to quantum mechanics, time might not exist in the way we perceive it—it could be just a human-made construct to measure change.

◎ There's an actual "Time Traveler Convention" that happened in 2005. Scientists at MIT hosted the event, inviting time travelers from the future to show up. No confirmed time travelers attended, but some believe they just chose to stay hidden.

◎ The faster you travel, the more you experience time dilation. If you spent five years traveling near the speed of light, you might return to Earth to find that centuries had passed. This is the real-life science behind movies like *Interstellar*.

◎ In 1971, scientists flew atomic clocks on airplanes around the world. When the clocks returned, they were slightly behind their identical counterparts on the ground, proving that time moves slower at high speeds—just as Einstein predicted.

◎ A statue in Ecuador marks the "Center of Time." It sits on the equator, where the Earth spins the fastest. Some cultures believe it's a natural gateway between different time periods.

◎ The oldest known time capsule was buried in 1777 in Massachusetts. It contained newspapers, coins, and a silver plate. When it was opened in 2015, everything inside was still perfectly preserved.

◎ In 2004, a cell phone was found in an Austrian archaeological dig from the 13th century. It resembled an ancient clay tablet but had markings similar to a modern keypad. Some conspiracy theorists claimed it was proof of time travel, but experts believe it was a hoax.

◉ The idea of a time machine predates H.G. Wells' *The Time Machine*. Ancient Hindu texts describe a king who traveled to the heavens for a short time, only to return to Earth and find that hundreds of years had passed.

◉ The "Philadelphia Experiment" is an alleged U.S. military test in 1943 that reportedly made a Navy ship disappear—and reappear in a different location. Some say the ship traveled through time, but the story is widely considered a hoax.

◉ In 1895, a woman in a painting by Ferdinand Georg Waldmüller appears to be holding a smartphone. The artwork, *The Expected One*, shows her gazing at an object that looks suspiciously modern, sparking theories of accidental time travel.

◉ A man named Al Bielek claimed he was part of a secret U.S. government time travel project. He said he was sent to the year 2137, where he saw floating cities and a drastically altered map of the world. His story remains a bizarre but unverified legend.

◉ The concept of time zones didn't exist before the 19th century. Before that, every town had its own local time, meaning travelers had to constantly reset their clocks as they moved.

◉ If time travel to the past is possible, where are all the time travelers? The "Fermi Paradox" of time travel suggests that if people from the future could visit us, we should have already met them—but maybe they're just really good at hiding.

◉ The famous "time-traveling hipster" photo shows a man in 1941 wearing sunglasses and a hoodie, standing out from the crowd. Many believe it's proof of a time traveler, but experts say his clothing was all available in the '40s.

◉ According to some theories, déjà vu might be a glitch in time. Some scientists speculate that our brains momentarily misalign events, making us feel like we've already lived through a moment before.

◉ In 2008, a man was arrested in Switzerland for sneaking into a high-security particle accelerator. He claimed to be from the future, sent back to stop the Large Hadron Collider from destroying the world. He disappeared after being detained, fueling conspiracy theories.

◎ In the 1977, a TV news broadcast in the U.K. was interrupted by a voice claiming to be from the future. The message warned humanity to change its ways before it was too late. It was never traced to any known radio signal.

◎ The "Chronovisor" was a device allegedly built by a Vatican priest that could view past events. According to the story, it was used to watch historical moments like Jesus' crucifixion before mysteriously disappearing.

◎ Time slows down the closer you get to a massive object. If you lived near a black hole, you could watch the universe outside speed up while barely aging yourself.

◎ The Voyager 1 spacecraft, launched in 1977, is essentially a time capsule hurtling through space. It carries sounds and images of Earth, potentially to be discovered by extraterrestrials in the distant future— long after humanity is gone.

◎ A wormhole could theoretically allow for instant time travel. These hypothetical tunnels in space-time might connect distant points in time and space, but no one knows if they actually exist.

◎ The Mayans believed time was cyclical, not linear. Their calendar predicted repeating ages of civilization, leading to the misconception that the world would end in 2012—when in reality, it was just the end of one time cycle.

DOOMSDAY & PREPPING

⊚ The Svalbard Global Seed Vault, nicknamed the "Doomsday Vault," stores over a million seed varieties deep inside a mountain in the Arctic. It's designed to withstand nuclear war, earthquakes, and climate disasters, ensuring humanity can restart agriculture if necessary.

⊚ The U.S. government has an official doomsday plane called the E-4B Nightwatch. This heavily fortified Boeing 747 can stay airborne for days and is meant to serve as a mobile command center in the event of nuclear war.

⊚ Preppers use Mylar bags and oxygen absorbers to store food for decades. Properly sealed rice and beans can last over 30 years, making them a staple for long-term survival planning.

⊚ The "Doomsday Clock" isn't just symbolic—it's adjusted every year by atomic scientists to reflect global threats like nuclear war and climate change. As of 2024, it's set at 90 seconds to midnight, the closest to catastrophe in history.

⊚ Fallout shelters built in the 1950s were designed to sustain people for two weeks—the assumed time it would take for radiation levels to drop to survivable levels after a nuclear blast. Many of these shelters still exist, hidden beneath cities and schools.

◎ One of the largest private bunker in the world is located in South Dakota. Called Vivos xPoint, it consists of 575 former military bunkers converted into a self-sufficient underground community capable of housing 5,000 people.

◎ The U.S. government has secret underground bunkers, like the Raven Rock Mountain Complex, designed to keep high-ranking officials safe during catastrophic events. Known as the "Underground Pentagon," it's capable of running military operations in complete secrecy.

◎ In the event of a nuclear explosion, the "rule of sevens" helps estimate radiation danger: After seven hours, fallout radiation drops to 10%, after 49 hours to 1%, and after two weeks to 0.1% of its initial intensity.

◎ A well-stocked prepper pantry includes at least one gallon of water per person per day. In a long-term crisis, rainwater harvesting and purification systems become crucial for survival.

◎ The government has detailed contingency plans for asteroid impacts. NASA actively tracks near-Earth objects, and the DART mission successfully tested planetary defense by altering an asteroid's trajectory.

◎ Some preppers bury "survival caches" filled with food, medical supplies, and weapons in secret locations. These are meant as emergency resupply points in case they need to bug out unexpectedly.

◎ The longest-lasting food in a prepper's pantry is honey. As mentioned before, it never spoils because of its low moisture content and natural antibacterial properties—archaeologists have even found 3,000-year-old edible honey in Egyptian tombs.

◎ The United States maintains a massive food stockpile known as the Strategic National Stockpile. It contains emergency medical supplies, vaccines, and other essentials for disasters, including a potential bioterror attack.

◎ During the Cold War, the U.S. government considered hiding a doomsday vault inside a mountain to store American culture and knowledge. This project never materialized, but similar digital archives now exist in Arctic locations.

◎ The "blackout bag" or "get home bag" is a smaller emergency kit designed to help someone survive for 24-48 hours if stranded away from home. It typically contains water, food, a flashlight, a fire starter, and a map in case GPS fails.

◎ The U.S. Air Force operates a fleet of "doomsday submarines" known as Ohio-class SSBNs. These nuclear-armed submarines are designed to launch retaliatory strikes even if the surface world is destroyed.

◎ The Pentagon's Continuity of Operations Plan (COOP) ensures that, in the event of a national emergency, the government can still function. This includes relocating leaders to secret locations, such as Mount Weather in Virginia.

◎ NASA has contingency plans for space disasters, including what to do if an astronaut is stranded on Mars. A proposed "Mars Direct" plan would involve pre-sent supply caches to sustain a lost astronaut until rescue.

◎ The city of Helsinki, Finland, has a vast underground bunker system that can shelter over 900,000 people—almost its entire population. These spaces double as shopping malls, sports arenas, and parking garages during peacetime.

◎ In a true doomsday scenario, access to antibiotics could mean life or death. Some preppers stockpile fish antibiotics, which contain the same active ingredients as human versions but are legally available without a prescription.

◎ The concept of a "nuclear winter" was first modeled in the 1950s, predicting that firestorms from nuclear blasts would send soot into the atmosphere, blocking sunlight for months or even years. This could lead to mass starvation even for those far from the blasts.

◎ Many preppers rely on HAM radios for emergency communication. Unlike cell phones and the internet, radio waves don't require infrastructure, making them a crucial tool if modern networks collapse.

◎ A common survivalist rule is the "Rule of Three": You can survive three minutes without air, three hours without shelter in extreme conditions, three days without water, and three weeks without food.

◎ The "nuclear triad" refers to a country's ability to launch nuclear weapons from land, air, and sea. The U.S., Russia, and China all maintain full nuclear triads, ensuring their ability to strike even if one leg of their defense is destroyed.

◎ In 1961, a B-52 bomber accidentally dropped two hydrogen bombs over North Carolina. One of them nearly detonated—only a single safety switch prevented an explosion 250 times more powerful than Hiroshima.

◎ The world's largest doomsday prepping community, The Survival Condo Project, is built inside a former missile silo in Kansas. It offers luxury underground apartments with renewable food and water supplies, costing millions per unit.

◎ EMP (Electromagnetic Pulse) attacks are a major concern for preppers, as they could wipe out power grids and electronics instantly. Some preppers build Faraday cages—shielded containers that block electromagnetic fields—to protect their devices.

◎ Some people believe Yellowstone's supervolcano is the ultimate doomsday scenario. A full eruption could cover the U.S. in ash, trigger a mini ice age, and make agriculture impossible for years. Scientists, however, estimate the odds of this happening anytime soon are very low.

◎ In a long-term disaster, bartering could replace traditional money. Many preppers stockpile tradeable goods like alcohol, coffee, batteries, and medical supplies in case currency becomes useless.

CRAZY ART

◎ In 1958, artist Yves Klein sold invisible art for gold. He called it *Zones of Immaterial Pictorial Sensibility* and gave buyers a receipt for their purchase. Most buyers ceremonially burned their receipts—completing Klein's artistic vision that art exists beyond the physical world.

◎ The world's largest painting, *The Journey of Humanity*, measures over 17,000 square feet. Created by artist Sacha Jafri in 2020, the piece was auctioned for $62 million, making it one of the most expensive artworks by a living artist. The entire canvas was painted inside a ballroom over seven months.

◎ Salvador Dalí once arrived at an art lecture wearing a deep-sea diving suit. As he spoke, he began suffocating because he hadn't connected the air supply properly. The audience thought it was part of the performance until assistants rushed to remove the helmet.

◎ Artist Piero Manzoni sold sealed cans of his own excrement in 1961, calling the work *Artist's Shit*. Each can was priced by weight to match the value of gold at the time. Decades later, some cans exploded due to internal gas buildup, proving that art truly has an expiration date.

◎ In 2019, artist Maurizio Cattelan taped a banana to a gallery wall and sold it for $120,000. Titled *Comedian*, the artwork sparked debate over what counts as art. When another artist ate the banana, the gallery simply replaced it with a new one—preserving the "concept" rather than the object itself.

◎ The Mona Lisa was once stolen by an Italian handyman who believed it should be returned to Italy. In 1911, Vincenzo Peruggia hid inside the Louvre overnight and walked out with the painting under his coat. The theft increased the painting's fame, turning it into the most recognized artwork in the world.

◎ Vincent van Gogh only sold one painting during his lifetime, *The Red Vineyard*, for about $2,000 in today's money. Today, his works sell for tens of millions, and his *Portrait of Dr. Gachet* once held the record for the most expensive painting ever sold at auction.

◎ In 1953, artist Robert Rauschenberg erased a drawing by legendary artist Willem de Kooning and titled the piece *Erased de Kooning Drawing*. The act itself was considered an artwork, questioning whether destruction could be a form of creation.

◎ The "Inkblot" paintings of Jackson Pollock, which appear chaotic, follow mathematical fractal patterns similar to those found in nature. Researchers found that Pollock's drip technique mimicked patterns seen in coastlines, clouds, and galaxies.

◎ In 2011, British artist Damien Hirst created a diamond-encrusted skull titled *For the Love of God*. The piece used over 8,600 diamonds and cost $20 million to produce. It was listed for sale at $100 million, though rumors suggest it was never actually sold.

◎ A 17th-century painting once attributed to an unknown artist was discovered in a farmhouse and later confirmed to be a lost Caravaggio. Originally bought for $1,500, it was valued at over $170 million after authentication. The owners had no idea they had a masterpiece in their attic.

◎ French artist Marcel Duchamp submitted a signed urinal as an art piece in 1917, titled *Fountain*. The work was rejected from an exhibition, but it later became one of the most influential pieces of modern art. It challenged traditional notions of what art could be, inspiring the conceptual art movement.

◎ In 2018, a painting by Banksy self-destructed seconds after being sold at auction for $1.4 million. Hidden inside the frame was a shredder that cut half of the painting into strips. The stunt only increased the artwork's value, and it was later renamed *Love is in the Bin*.

◎ Artist Chris Burden once had himself shot in the arm as part of a performance art piece called *Shoot* in 1971. The stunt was meant to comment on gun violence and the Vietnam War. He later admitted he didn't fully anticipate how painful it would be.

◎ Leonardo da Vinci's *The Last Supper* was once used as a doorway. In the 17th century, monks cut a hole in the bottom of the famous painting to make room for a door. The damage permanently erased Jesus' feet from the mural.

◎ The Statue of Liberty's color-changing transformation from copper to green was entirely unplanned. When gifted by France in 1886, the statue had a shiny bronze appearance. Over the years, oxidation turned the copper surface into the familiar green patina seen today.

◎ Some of Pablo Picasso's paintings contain hidden artworks underneath them. Infrared scans have revealed that he often reused canvases, painting over earlier works. In one famous case, his masterpiece *The Blue Room* was found to have a completely different portrait beneath it.

◎ A street artist once painted an entire bridge in France to look like it was crumbling into pieces. The illusion was so realistic that some pedestrians hesitated to cross it. The work used anamorphic perspective, a technique that makes 2D art appear 3D from a specific viewpoint.

◎ The paint used in *Starry Night* by Vincent van Gogh actually glows under UV light. Researchers found that the pigments in his paintings have unique chemical properties that make them react differently to various lighting conditions.

⊚ The Louvre was once used as a prison. Long before it became the world's most famous museum, the building housed political prisoners in medieval France. It didn't officially become a public art museum until the French Revolution.

⊚ The paint used in Egyptian tombs has remained vibrant for thousands of years because of an unusual ingredient: crushed gemstones. Ancient artists mixed ground-up minerals like lapis lazuli into their paint to create long-lasting colors.

⊚ Michelangelo secretly hid anatomical drawings inside the Sistine Chapel ceiling. Scholars believe that God's cloak in *The Creation of Adam* contains a hidden outline of the human brain, possibly representing the divine gift of intelligence.

⊚ In 2010, an artist placed a golden toilet titled *America* in a museum, and it was fully functional. Created by Maurizio Cattelan, the 18-karat toilet was meant as a commentary on wealth and excess. It was later stolen in a daring heist and remains missing.

⊚ The Eiffel Tower was almost turned into an apartment building. Before its completion, artist Gustave Eiffel designed a private apartment at the top. He used it as a personal retreat, and it still exists today as a small museum.

⊚ There's a secret room behind Mount Rushmore, hidden inside Abraham Lincoln's head. Originally designed as a Hall of Records, it contains historical documents sealed in a titanium vault. Tourists can't access it, making it one of America's most mysterious artistic features.

⊚ The "Blackest Black" paint, Vantablack, absorbs 99.96% of light, making objects coated in it appear like a void. Artist Anish Kapoor secured exclusive rights to use it, sparking outrage in the art community. In response, another artist, Stuart Semple, created *The Pinkest Pink*— available to everyone except Kapoor.

⊚ The famous "Screaming Man" in Edvard Munch's *The Scream* was inspired by a real-life moment. Munch described feeling an overwhelming sense of existential dread while walking at sunset, leading him to capture the emotion in paint. The eerie sky in the painting was likely influenced by the aftermath of a volcanic eruption.

◎ A Salvador Dalí painting was once stolen in broad daylight from a New York gallery. The thief simply walked in, took *Cartel de Don Juan Tenorio* off the wall, and left. The painting was later mailed back anonymously in a bizarre twist.

◎ The largest sculpture in the world is the *Spring Temple Buddha* in China, standing 502 feet tall—nearly twice the height of the Statue of Liberty. Built in 2008, it was designed to withstand earthquakes and typhoons. The entire project took over a decade to complete.

Enjoyed the book?

Scan the QR code below to leave a review! Your feedback helps me create even more amazing books. Thank you for your support!

http://geni.us/BenDouglas

CONCLUSION

And there you have it—a collection of fascinating, weird, and downright unbelievable facts from across history, pop culture, science, and beyond. Whether you've been amazed, amused, or even slightly horrified, I hope this book has sparked your curiosity and given you plenty of conversation starters (or at least some fun facts to drop at awkward silences).

Trivia isn't just about knowing random facts—it's about seeing the world from new angles. The stories behind the facts often reveal incredible human achievements, bizarre coincidences, and the kind of details that make life far more interesting than fiction. So next time you hear a piece of trivia, don't just take it at face value—dig deeper, question it, and who knows? You might uncover an even better story hiding underneath.

If you enjoyed this book, don't stop here! There's always more to discover, whether it's in the pages of history, the depths of science, or the strange corners of pop culture. So keep exploring, keep asking questions, and most importantly—keep having fun with it. After all, life's too short not to fill it with fascinating facts.

TURN THE PAGE FOR A FREE BONUS BOOK!

CLAIM YOUR FREE GIFT!

Scan the QR code below to download your free bonus gift!

Or go to
http://geni.us/TriviaBonus